Praise for
Building a Business with a Beat

"I love this inspiring book and so will you. A classic servant leader, Judi Sheppard Missett's passion and purpose for 50 years has been helping people reach their fitness and entrepreneurial goals while having fun, making friends, and listening to positive, energizing music. Here, Judi generously shares the challenges and victories, problems and solutions of a little startup business that grew into a global brand. The Jazzercise success story is a great read—and a shot in the arm for leaders, entrepreneurs, and fitness enthusiasts everywhere. Read this book and get moving toward your goals—whatever they may be!"

—Ken Blanchard, coauthor of
The New One Minute Manager® and *Servant Leadership in Action*

"This book is informative, inspiring and empowering—not just about building a business with a beat, but about building a life with a heart." —Dr. Art Ulene,
former NBC TODAY Show Medical Correspondent

"Today's modern fitness movement owes a debt of gratitude to Judi, who has been an innovator for half a century. She exemplified early what a purpose driven business is. Fans and newbies alike will enjoy and benefit from this book."

—Christie Hefner, former Chairman and CEO of
Playboy Enterprises and cofounder of the Committee of 200

"Judi Sheppard Missett has indeed built an empire and is a rock star in the world of women's entrepreneurship. She leads with sound business principles, a kind heart, and a true love for the amazing business she and her team have grown over five decades. This book is a must-read." —Monica Smiley,
Editor and Publisher of *Enterprising Women Magazine*

"I am so proud to have Judi Sheppard Missett as a WPO member, Board director, friend and one of my personal heroes. She rebelled by taking a nontraditional path, doing what she loved and building it into a fitness empire. Her commitment to making a difference has helped raise $30 million for charity. A gracious and supportive leader, Judi is always willing to share her wisdom with others and pay it forward for the next generation of women entrepreneurs. She emulates our organization's motto: Reaching Farther. Together."

—Dr. Marsha Firestone, Founder and President of Women Presidents' Organization

"Judi was lovingly called 'The Diamond' by my father, Gus, because of her brilliant spark. She shined in every way—talented, creative, passionate, intelligent, generous and determined. Judi's vision is the reason JAZZERCISE, INC. changed the exercise world!"

—Amy Giordano, Executive Director of Gus Giordano Dance School

"Judi Sheppard Missett has been an extraordinary, innovative leader in the business of health and fitness for 50 years. Not only is she a pioneer in the industry, but also an incredible visionary who still creates, leads and inspires to this day. By working with Judi at the National Fitness Leaders Association, the California Governor's Council on Physical Fitness and Sports, and the Great American Workout at the White House, I have always admired how she leads with heart, soul, passion, and kindness. It was an enormous honor to present Judi with the well-deserved President's Council on Physical Fitness and Sports Lifetime Achievement Award. Her commitment to excellence goes hand-in-hand with fun and pure enjoyment. She leads Jazzercise with a culture of philanthropy, always giving back. The way Judi combines her remarkable business acumen with serving others is a wonderful example for any aspiring leader."

—Melissa Johnson, MS, former Executive Director of President's Council on Physical Fitness and Sports

"Judi's enthusiasm, healthy lifestyle, and business insight have created a fitness empire that has had worldwide impact."

—John Cates, former Executive Director of
CA Governor's Council on Physical Fitness and Sports

"Judi Sheppard Missett is an icon in the fitness industry. She was a pioneer of dance-exercise that helped launch an entire worldwide fitness movement! She figured out how to make fitness fun (and effective) and has set an example for the rest of the industry to follow. She has been a role model for many, including us. IDEA gave her many awards over the years, including the Lifetime Achievement award. Judi is one in a million!"

—Kathie and Peter Davis, cofounders of
IDEA Health and Fitness Association

BUILDING A
Business
WITH A
Beat

Leadership Lessons from **Jazzercise**—
An Empire Built on **Passion, Purpose, and Heart**

Judi Sheppard Missett
JAZZERCISE Founder and CEO

with Susan Carol McCarthy

New York Chicago San Francisco Athens London Madrid
Mexico City Milan New Delhi Singapore Sydney Toronto

1 2 3 4 5 6 7 8 9   QVS 24 23 22 21 20 19

ISBN 978-1-260-44130-7
MHID 1-260-44130-X

e-ISBN 978-1-260-44131-4
e-MHID 1-260-44131-8

Library of Congress Cataloging-in-Publication Data

Names: Missett, Judi Sheppard, 1944– author. | McCarthy, Susan Carol, author.
Title: Building a business with a beat : leadership lessons from Jazzercise : an empire
    built on passion, purpose, and heart / Judi Sheppard Missett, Jazzercise founder &
    CEO, with Susan Carol McCarthy.
Description: New York : McGraw-Hill Education, [2019]
Identifiers: LCCN 2019010687 (print) | LCCN 2019013519 (ebook) |
    ISBN 9781260441314 () | ISBN 1260441318 () | ISBN 9781260441307
    (hardback) | ISBN 126044130X
Subjects: LCSH: Small business—Growth. | Success in business. | New
    business enterprises. | Jazzercise, Inc. | BISAC: BUSINESS & ECONOMICS /
    Entrepreneurship.
Classification: LCC HD2341 (ebook) | LCC HD2341 .M573 2019 (print) |
    DDC 658.4/21—dc23 LC record available at https://lccn.loc.gov/2019010687

For Skyla and Sienna, Shanna and Brendan,
my parents June and Del Sheppard,
my dear Jack,
and
passionate Jazzercise people—
past, present, and future—everywhere

Jazzercise Timeline

1969
Judi Sheppard Missett conceives a dance fitness class that evolves into Jazzercise in Chicago, Illinois.

1972
The Missett family moves to northern San Diego County, California. Judi begins to teach classes at the La Jolla YMCA and Oceanside Parks and Recreation.

1977
Judi holds the first workshops to train instructors.

Jazzercise opens their corporate office in Carlsbad, California.

1979
Jazzercise goes international with classes in Europe, Brazil, and Japan.

1980
Jazzertogs by Jazzercise is established, offering a complete line of fitness apparel, activewear, fitness accessories, Jazzercise DVDs, and logo merchandise.

1981
Judi begins hosting a segment on weekly entertainment news program "PM Magazine."

1982
Jazzercise offers its first franchises.

First Jazzercise International Instructors' Convention.

1983
Jazzercise takes its foothold in all 50 United States.

1984
The first Jazzercise home workout videocassette, titled *Jazzercise*, goes gold with 25,000 copies sold.

Jazzercise performs in the Opening Ceremonies of the Los Angeles Olympics before a TV audience of 2.5 billion viewers.

1986
President Ronald Reagan names Judi "Top Woman Entrepreneur."

1989
The Los Angeles Times Syndicate invites Judi to write an internationally syndicated fitness column on their behalf.

Judi teaches the world's largest aerobic dance class to 6,000 Jazzercise customers at JazzerJam Chicago '89.

1991
President George Bush and Arnold Schwarzenegger invite Judi to participate in the "Great American Workout" at the White House.

Ernst & Young Inc., Merrill Lynch, and the Union-Tribune Publishing Company honor Judi as the "San Diego Female Entrepreneur of the Year."

1992
Judi is inducted into the IDEA Hall of Fame.

Jazzercise Kids Get Fit program reaches 402,000 children worldwide and is presented to the President's Council on Physical Fitness and Sports with Arnold Schwarzenegger.

1999

The world's largest Jazzercise benefit for breast cancer research is held, raising more than $1.2 million.

Judi is honored as a March of Dimes 1999 Mother of the Year in San Diego, California.

2007

Judi is an inaugural recipient of the Lifetime Achievement Award from the President's Council on Physical Fitness and Sports.

2008

Judi joined a select group of women U.S. political and business leaders for the Stellar Women's Leadership Delegation to China.

2009

Jazzercise signs on "Dancing with the Stars" two-time champion Cheryl Burke as company's first celebrity spokesperson to star in national advertising campaign.

Jazzercise 40th Anniversary celebrated in Chicago as the company doubles in size.

2010

Shanna Missett Nelson is named President of Jazzercise, Inc.

2011

Jazzercise ranks #1 fitness franchise on prestigious *Entrepreneur* Magazine Franchise 500.

2012

Jazzercise ranks #1 on the *San Diego Business Journal*'s list of top 50 women-owned businesses in San Diego County.

2014

Judi is honored with the Entrepreneurial Champion Luminary Award by the Committee of 200 (C200).

Judi is named *San Diego Magazine*'s "Woman of the Year."

Guinness World Record set for largest Junior Jazzercise lesson at Jazzercise Live! Hiroshima.

2016

Judi is chosen as part of a select group of women leaders to attend the "United State of Women," a White-House sponsored conference in Washington, D.C.

Along with 39 other entrepreneurs, scientists, and social leaders, Judi is named to the *Union-Tribune* "40 San Diegans Who Changed the World."

2017

Judi receives The Gus Giordano Jazz Legacy Foundation, Gus Legacy Award.

San Diego Business Journal and Union Bank award Judi and Jazzercise Inc. with Women of the Year and Lifetime Achievement Awards.

2018

Judi receives Enterprising Women's Legacy Award.

Jazzercise global cumulative sales top $2 billion.

2019

Judi releases her book *Building a Business with a Beat* with Susan Carol McCarthy.

Jazzercise celebrates "50 Years Strong" with an international convention in San Diego, California with attendees from around the world.

Carlsbad Chamber of Commerce honors Judi with Lifetime Achievement Award.

CONTENTS

PART ONE
    FIND THE BEAT   1

    CHAPTER 1   Beginnings   3
    CHAPTER 2   Listen. Trust. Act.   25
    CHAPTER 3   Expect Resistance.
    Do It Anyway.   39

PART TWO
    MAINTAIN YOUR RHYTHM THROUGH
    GROWTH AND CHANGE   55

    CHAPTER 4   Watch for Cues, Signs,
    and Signals   57
    CHAPTER 5   Growing Organically, Going
    Viral . . . and Global   77
    CHAPTER 6   Be a Rebel   105
    CHAPTER 7   Hard Yeses, Flexible Nos, and
    the Magical Power of *Why Not?*   119
    CHAPTER 8   Create a Purposeful Culture   141
    CHAPTER 9   Cultivate Your Customer
    Community   159
    CHAPTER 10   Assessing Expectations,
    Maintaining Excellence   175

CHAPTER 11   The Joy of Giving Back   193

CHAPTER 12   Secrets to Our Longevity   211

PART THREE

HARMONIZE YOUR BODY, MIND,
AND SPIRIT   229

CHAPTER 13   Make the Body-Mind-Spirit
Connection   231

CHAPTER 14   Keep Moving Forward   247

NOTE TO MY GRANDDAUGHTERS   255

ACKNOWLEDGMENTS   257

INDEX   261

PART ONE
FIND THE BEAT

Everything in the universe has rhythm, everything dances.
—Maya Angelou

You get that right tickin' rhythm, man, and it's ON!
—Fats Waller

There are elements of music, especially jazz music, that I found instructive to building a business, or a life, with a beat.
—Judi Sheppard Missett

CHAPTER 1

Beginnings

Work with what you've got to find your passion. Pay attention to your earliest mentors, then be prepared to dance your ass off.

[signature]

THE PIGEON-TOED TODDLER

My mother had two stories she liked to tell about my baby-hood. The first one goes like this: I was born severely pigeon-toed, with both feet and ankles turned inward. It was cute enough on a newborn. But when I began to take my first steps, it gave me an awkward, unsteady gait. My mother was a young navy wife living in base housing in San Diego, while Dad was on a ship fighting World War II in the Pacific. When she took me for a first-year checkup, she quizzed the navy doctor for a way to correct my stance. Common practice back then was a pair of special shoes anchored to an iron bar pressing the feet into a more outward position. "But I've also heard dance classes can help," the doctor said.

> *"I've heard dance classes can help."*
>
> —Pediatrician at the Naval Medical Center in San Diego

The shoe setup was free from the navy hospital, but dance classes were not, so each night, for a while, she'd slip my feet into the white leather shoes whose soles were firmly attached to a metal bar six inches apart. She'd lace the shoes securely up to my ankles, lay me on my back in my crib, both feet forced apart, and try not to listen to me cry. This lasted a few months, after which, with no discernable improvement, my mom put an end to our "nightly torture."

Her second story involved a favorite pastime of wartime navy wives—strolling and window-shopping among the charming streets and shops of Coronado Island, across the bay from downtown San Diego. It was fun, she said, and it was free. One day, on Isabelle Avenue, she spotted a sign that read JEANNE JURAD DANCE STUDIO, ALL TYPES OF DANCING FOR ALL AGES, and decided to investigate. The small reception room was empty. While she looked around for a flyer, her 18-month-old toddler wandered down the hall toward an open door and the sound of music. Watching and listening, I lifted my arms and began to swing and sway in the doorway. Someone stepped out of the room and called to my mother, "You should get this girl into dance classes. She's got some talent!" Whoever you were, thank you.

When my father was discharged from the navy in late 1946, we moved back to southwest Iowa, where both my parents had been raised. Red Oak, Iowa, population 5,763, was the county seat of Montgomery County, with a town square just like the one in the movie *Back to the Future*, surrounded by acres of farms and cornfields.

My dad, Del Sheppard, had a deep, resonant voice, which earned him a job as an announcer on the local Creston radio station. He also worked nights part-time for the Red Oak Police Department. I was always thrilled to hear him on the radio or see him in a police car around town. Later, he went to work for much better pay at the Iowa Soil Conservation Commission, which unfortunately required a lot of traveling around the state.

Our new home in a new neighborhood wasn't large by Red Oak standards, but its two bedrooms plus attic and basement were spacious compared to naval housing. Its exterior was white clapboard, and my mother's first order of business was to paint the front door and window shutters powder blue, in tribute to her 100 percent Swedish heritage.

Her second order of business was to find a dance studio offering lessons for three-year-olds. Fortunately, she found 21-year-old Joan Leavitt, who was then splitting her teaching time between nearby Shenandoah and a larger studio in (one-hour-away) Council Bluffs.

Proof of Joan's local popularity is in my first recital program for "Joan Leavitt presents VARIETY SHOW" at the Shenandoah High School Auditorium on June 1–2, 1948. Thirty-two different dance numbers were performed by 102 students on two nights in a row. Among them, four-year-old Judy Ann Sheppard danced "Sweet Miss, Dainty Miss" in an orchid ruffled dress made by her mother.

MY FIRST MENTOR

Although my mother was delighted that dancing helped normalize my stance, she never pushed me to dance. In fact, on several occasions when I became frustrated and com-

> *"If you can't put your heart into it, find something else and do that."*
>
> ⸺My mother, June Nelson Sheppard

plained about a particular dance move, sequence, or challenge, she told me explicitly, "Look, if this isn't something you want to do, then stop. Find something else you can put your heart into and do that." Knowing I had the freedom to take a different path at any time made it easier to keep going. She also made it clear that, if I was going to continue, I had to practice. Often, she practiced with me. She believed in the importance of working hard to refine talent rather than simply relying on it.

For the next seven years, I worked hard on my dancing and have three large scrapbooks of recital programs, county fair performances, and appearance flyers to prove it. In my eleventh summer, however, my teacher Joan Leavitt decided that her duties in both Council Bluffs and Shenandoah were too much for her, and she elected to pull back into her Council Bluffs studio, an hour away.

My mother, however, was not to be deterred. On her own, she made the rounds of every major dance studio in both Council Bluffs and Omaha, across the Missouri River, with the ingenious proposal that if they or an assistant would consider teaching satellite classes twice a week in Red Oak, she would find an appropriate venue, recruit the required number of students, help produce and promote an annual recital, and handle all the accounting! Most of the big-city studio owners passed. But after numerous tries, my mother found a few talented teachers who were willing to "give it a try."

With true entrepreneurial zeal, once she'd secured several local sites, Mom made up flyers for various classes—ballet, tap, lyrical, and jazz (my favorite), as well as folk and social dancing—and posted them at nursery schools, churches, libraries, and grocery stores around Red Oak and in all the smaller farm communities within a 20-mile radius. Her efforts were an impressive success.

Two years later, when I was only 13, several little girls in the neighborhood approached me to ask if I would be their teacher. I talked to my parents about the possibility. They quizzed me extensively about my objectives, my willingness to commit for no less than a nine-month (September through June) period, and the need to mount a recital at the end. When they were convinced that—whether I succeeded or failed—this could be a good learning experience for me, my father remodeled our basement into a small studio. And once again, my mother went to work, this time helping her daughter set up and manage the business. I began with eight students in September 1957 and mounted our first small recital that Christmas. By June, I had 100 students and a sold-out two-night recital in Red Oak High School's auditorium.

My dad created the space for me to teach my students, and my mom helped me with the books and drove me downtown every Monday to deposit my weekend earnings in the bank "for college." But they also insisted that I was in charge; that whatever decisions I made had consequences; and that owning, correcting, and learning from my mistakes were the keys to real success. Years later, when I decided to start my own dance fitness business in Chicago, I remembered what my mother had done. I knew the model worked. I knew I could develop a program that would help women achieve their fitness goals, build their own businesses, support one another, and feel good doing it. She taught me to be an entrepreneur.

Over all those years, I watched my mother tackle problems and create solutions on the fly. When the National Guard called at the last minute to say they needed the Armory, where dance classes were held, for weekend maneuvers, she immediately called the Oddfellows Hall to access their empty-on-Saturday-nights second floor for dance classes and notified all the students of the change. She never had a formal "plan" and didn't let that stop her. Her mantra was "Why not?" She didn't indulge in self-doubt. She simply felt "all you can do is your best. After that, just keep moving forward." She believed in herself and she believed in me. That confidence took root. And it gave me faith in myself and others.

MY FIRST DANCE MENTOR

My earliest memory is the dusty, musty smell of the floor in the Shenandoah National Guard Armory combined with the sheer joy of dancing in Joan's and my first local dance classes. Eventually dancing—and maybe just getting older—corrected my "pigeon-toed" problem. Twice-weekly classes with other dance-loving children helped me cope with my innate shyness. And, over time, Joan's enthusiastic teaching and innovative choreography helped me discover the passion for jazz dance that sustains me to this day.

Joan was endlessly creative and, as evidenced by more than 14 years of dance recital programs, she never repeated herself. Her routines were always fresh, fun to dance, and entertaining to watch. Through Joan's tireless efforts, I was able to master the fundamental moves of ballet, tap, lyrical, and acrobatic jazz and grasp the basics of choreography.

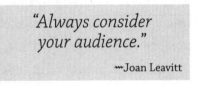

"Always consider your audience."

⸺Joan Leavitt

In the summer of 1956, Joan suggested I might enjoy competing in the four-state dance contest that was a part of Tabor, South Dakota's celebration called Czech Days. By that time, we had both discovered that I was apparently born with extreme flexibility. (In the old days, the term was *double jointed*; today it's called hypermobility.) In essence, I could do things a lot of dancers couldn't, like run up the wall and back-flip into the splits, or bend over backward, grab my ankles, and walk across the room. That second move earned me the nickname "the Upside-Down Girl." For Czech Days, Joan choreographed a lyrical dance that fused ballet, tap, and jazz. To match the mood of the dance, my mother designed and made a very pretty, short yet elegant white dress. I won second place and was not happy. I wanted first place.

The following year, Joan taught me an important lesson. "Look, since the folks in South Dakota weren't exactly wowed by the lyrical stuff," she said, "this time, let's use your special skills and knock their socks off." Her idea was to have my dad construct a large wooden drum, which became a prop to tap dance on, backflip off, and support a jazzy series of acrobatic backbends, elbow stands, and splits. My costume was a sparkly, sequined leotard. The crowd was definitely wowed and gave me my first-ever standing ovation. And the judges awarded me the grand prize—35 silver dollars in a gold-toned trophy cup! "Always consider your audience," Joan insisted. And the good people of Tabor, South Dakota, proved she was right.

After Joan's decision to end her local classes and concentrate on her Council Bluffs studio, even after I had students of my own, our relationship continued through private classes in Council Bluffs, workshops in Omaha, and referrals to other advanced teachers in both cities for special training.

Joan's lesson—always consider your audience—was repeated throughout the years I trained with her. The summer before I entered Red Oak High School, the band director contacted me to ask if I'd consider forming a troupe of dancing majorettes to march ahead of the band in parades and perform at halftime shows on the football field. I was thrilled to be invited but hesitant to accept. Twirling a baton was not in my skill set. But Joan had another student, Mary Jean Tibbels, who had been Nebraska's state twirling champion three years earlier. She put us together and, while Mary Jean and I worked hard on my twirling abilities, Joan suggested several ideas for crowd-pleasing, mostly dancing, halftime routines. When I despaired that I'd never be as good a twirler as Mary Jean, Joan waved off my objections, one hand perpetually holding a small green bottle of Coke and a lit cigarette. "You'll never be Mary Jean," she said. "But as Judy, you've got first-class style, grace, long legs that can high-step strut with the best of them, and the personality to sell whatever you do!" The Red Oak High Dancing Majorettes became so popular, we were invited to perform at other schools, parades, and county fairs.

Between my junior and senior years, Joan and Mary Jean urged me to compete in a nationwide contest sponsored by the National Baton Twirling Association for "America's Most Beautiful Majorette." I hesitated once again. Though my twirling skills had improved, they were hardly at a national award-winning level. Like before, however, Joan assured me that other elements of my performance could compensate. Plus, "I've got a great idea!" Since I was from Iowa, Joan's idea to help make my performance more memorable for the judges was to top both tips of my baton with an ear of corn and twirl to the state song, "See yonder's field of tasseled corn, Iowa, O! Iowa." My mother's contribution was a leafy green costume with a yellow sequined bodice that mimicked corn kernels. Potentially crowd-pleasing concepts, for sure; but do you have any idea how much two ears of corn alter the spin on a slim-shaft baton? I never worked so hard in my life. But

Joan's instinct was right again. The judges found the corn-cob-twirling girl from Iowa unforgettable, and I was crowned America's Most Beautiful Majorette, circa 1961.

Beyond bragging rights, the title came with the opportunity to teach a one-week twirling and dance clinic at Missouri State Teachers College and attend the one-week Young and Beautiful Charm Camp hosted by the University of Mississippi in Oxford, in sweltering mid-July. At Charm Camp, I learned such crucially important tips as "Never, never stand erect when brushing your hair. For the full stimulating effect, bend over from the waist and let your hair dangle." Also, "A woman's bust should be 12 inches larger than her waist."

Of course, the contest was a public relations and publicity vehicle for the National Baton Twirling Association and, unbeknownst to me, they sent a press release and photo of me doing a high kick to every conceivable news outlet. One newspaper, the US Army's *Stars and Stripes,* ran the photo with caption that practically took up a full page. For weeks afterward, I received letters from soldiers all over the world, addressed simply to "Judy Sheppard, Red Oak, IA," asking me to write them back, if they could be my boyfriend, or if they might come visit me when they were home on leave. As far as I know, my father answered every one of them.

That whirlwind summer I also received letters from several college band directors asking me to consider their campus and band in my future plans. I answered each of those, hoping for some sort of scholarship. However, in those long-ago, pre–Title IX days, there were no scholarships available for majorettes. But they would be happy to have me pay for "the honor" of adding my talents to their band program.

When I returned from Charm Camp, Joan had another surprise in store for me. Gus Giordano, the former Broadway dancer, choreographer, and famed artistic director of Gus Giordano Jazz Dance Chicago,

"Don't forget to have fun."

⁓Joan Leavitt

was coming to Omaha to teach an advanced class and she had arranged for me to attend. This introduction— during which Gus suggested, "If you haven't made up your mind yet, why not consider Northwestern University in Evanston? My studio is there, too"—changed my life.

Even now, it's hard to calculate the many ways Joan Leavitt helped me change and grow. I danced with her from the time I was three until I left Red Oak for college at age 18. She taught me the foundations of dance as well as the basic principles of choreography, both of which Gus Giordano would later help me polish. She served as the necessary yin to my parents' yang. By that I mean, Joan balanced my mother's practicality, my father's protectivity, and their joint emphasis on hard

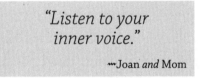

"Listen to your inner voice."

⁓Joan *and* Mom

work, perseverance, and strict economy with her sense of the joyful expansiveness of dance, her theatrical flair, and her demand for the inclusion of fun in every class and performance. Without Joan, one of the core elements of Jazzercise—that fitness can be fun—might never have occurred to me.

Although my mother and Joan were quite different, at the core these two strong women shared a fundamental truth. While my mother would say, "Follow your heart," Joan's version was, "You gotta go with your gut." Both were right and also encouraged me from my earliest memory to "listen to that inner voice; it will *never* steer you wrong."

MY JAZZ DANCE MASTER

In the fall of 1962, my parents and I left Red Oak and drove north to Evanston and Chicago. Essentially, we were retracing in reverse the same route my Swedish immigrant grandpa, Axel Nelson, traveled to begin his new life in Iowa. For my new life in Chicago, I had a trunk full of clothes, shoes, and supplies; a dorm room at Northwestern University; a full load of college classes; plus, the very exciting opportunity to study with jazz

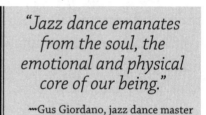

"Jazz dance emanates from the soul, the emotional and physical core of our being."

⸺Gus Giordano, jazz dance master

dance master Gus Giordano. Between my savings and my parents' contribution, I had enough money for basics and the possibility (fingers crossed) of work through the three-story Evanston studios of Giordano Jazz Dance Chicago, the first studio in America dedicated solely to jazz dance.

On that crisp autumn day, I felt on my own . . . and on my way! So much so that, somewhere between the quiet ripening heartlands surrounding Red Oak and the throbbing beat of Chicago, I decided to change my name from Judy with a *y* to Judi with an *i*. My birth name was Judith, so it wasn't unjustified. But that small change was my own private declaration of independence. It sounded more adult and more sophisticated to me—sexier, too, though Lord knows I had yet to discover what *that* was all about.

The "Giordano technique" of jazz dance was a revelation. Unlike other forms of dance, which he considered "more cranial/coming from the head," jazz dance, Gus explained, "emanates from the soul, the emotional and physical core of our being." A big part of Gus's practice involved isolating body parts, such as the pelvis, the spine, or the rib cage, so they appear to move separately from the rest of the body. "What a ballet dancer does as one arm movement," he said, "we do as five or six parts." To me, Gus's style was challenging, precise, and full of pent-up passion. I loved it!

> *"Create an emotional journey, with a beginning, middle, and end."*
> ⸺Gus Giordano

Many people didn't realize that Gus's degree from the University of Missouri was in both dance and creative writing. As a result, he approached each dance from a narrative perspective. "Jazz dance is not just a series of steps. It's a story, an emotional journey, with a beginning, middle, and end." The structure of every Jazzercise class—from the beginning warmup, to the middle building to high cardio, to the ending cool-down—was inspired by Gus's regimen and what you experience when you attend a theatrical performance.

In my freshman year, with Gus's encouragement, I auditioned for Northwestern's annual "WAA-MU Show," a large and popular song-and-dance review presented jointly by the Women's Athletic Association and the Men's Union. The cast historically comprised upperclassmen, but that year I became the first freshman ever asked to participate. As the cast rookie, I was assigned the nebulous role of "Showgirl." While others performed their one set piece and were done, I had many different, small backup parts in many different costumes. It was nerve-racking but beyond exciting. And it helped me catch the eye of an agent whom Gus had invited to attend.

For the next several years, both Gus and my theatrical agent, Shirley Hamilton, provided me with much-needed opportunities to earn extra income for unforeseen expenses. Through my agent, I was called out for newspaper and magazine modeling jobs, TV commercials, plus live demos at Chicago auto shows. Through Gus's side ventures—producing corporate, industrial, and theatrical dance shows—I auditioned and was cast in a wide variety of live weekend gigs, which didn't interfere with my weekday college classes.

At the time, industrial theater shows were a popular way for national companies to introduce a new product or product line to their local distributors at their annual Chicago convention. Instead of a boring sales speech outlining the virtues and benefits of a product, a performer would sing a catchy jingle about the product, or dance around to demonstrate it, or both.

My first audition for a major industrial show was in downtown Chicago. After riding the subway for the first time, overshooting my stop, and having to run back several blocks to the right address, I discovered that, once again, I was the youngest, least experienced "showgirl" there. The concept called for four young women to showcase a new Admiral television set and other appliances. Several obviously "pro" performers went ahead of me, which gave me time to catch my breath and calm myself with the thought, "Well, at least you won't have to twirl a baton with two corn cobs attached!"

When my turn came, I launched into my audition routine, gave it my all, and got the job! Later, the casting director shared with me that I reminded him of his

> *"Always consider your audience, part two: does what you're offering match what your audience is looking for?"*
>
> ⸺Note to self

wife. She was a dancer, too, with blond hair and very long legs. He wasn't hitting on me, but his comment reaffirmed Joan Leavitt's maxim: always consider your audience. It's never as simple as whether or not you have talent; it's also important how what you have to offer matches what your audience is looking for. This precept would surface again and serve me well in the earliest days of Jazzercise.

⁓

After the Admiral appliance show, I worked many more industrial theater shows, locally in Chicago, throughout the Midwest, and internationally for companies like Philco, Seagrams, Westinghouse, U.S. Steel, and Control Data.

In addition to corporate shows, Gus also produced and packaged theatrical dance shows for places like downtown Chicago's Gaslight Club. The concept was a roadshow hosted by high-end country clubs and other venues around the Midwest to provide them with an evening of 1920s-themed entertainment and promote the Gaslight as *the* club to visit when in Chicago. We were a cast of four female dancers—the Gaslight Girls—backed by a four-piece Dixieland jazz band. Dressed as flappers, we'd open dancing the Charleston to "C'mon, Get Happy!" Then there were several solos. Mine was "I Can't Give You Anything but Love, Baby!" Finally, we'd whip the crowd into a dance contest, award a bottle of champagne to the winners, and close with a rousing can-can version of "Chicago!" Those weekend Gaslight shows were probably my favorite gigs throughout my sophomore and junior years. Thanks to Gus, I was growing as both a person and a professional, and I was able to afford to stay at Northwestern and in Chicago.

MY FUTURE HUSBAND

Toward the end of my junior year, a dorm mate asked me to tag along on a blind date with a couple of Northwestern guys. With classes and studying on weekdays and performances

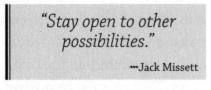

"Stay open to other possibilities."

—Jack Missett

most Friday and Saturday nights, I hadn't done much dating. "Why not?" I thought, and I agreed to go. Unfortunately, before the date came to pass, I was cast by Philco TVs and Appliance Group to entertain their top distributors and salespeople during six weeks of sales promotion awards trips in gorgeous Puerto Rico. We were a female quartet meant to jazz up various new product and sales presentations to the sales guys with such catchy lyrics as:

> *As you can see, I've got a chassis,*
> *Precision built and service free.*
> *I think that you will all agree*
> *That my chassis is classy,*
> *The best in TV!*

It was the mid-1960s, and very much like the TV show "Mad Men." Most of our audience were traveling with their wives on a well-deserved award trip. Although there were some bachelors in the bunch, who definitely tried to hit on us, we four girls had all signed contracts to "maintain professional decorum at all times." For the most part, we took that seriously.

While we were there, Puerto Rico celebrated an annual holiday that they claimed was "bigger than New Year's Eve." Called La Noche de San Juan, it was the June 24 birthday celebration of the island's patron saint, John the Baptist. It was basically a big beach party capped off at midnight with the tradition of walking then falling backward into the ocean three times. Their belief was that the water cleanses you of any bad luck and you'd be blessed with good luck in the coming year. Did it work? Well, you can decide once you hear what happened next.

After I returned to Chicago, my girlfriend rescheduled the blind date I'd missed by going to Puerto Rico. His name was Jack Missett and we agreed to go out to the Thumbs Up

Club on Chicago's North Side. The Thumbs Up was home to the fantastic blues band Baby Huey & the Babysitters. The crowd was in awe of the Babysitters' funky, full-throttle showmanship—and of 300-pound Baby Huey Ramey's stunning dance moves. This guy's dancing was phenomenal. And Jack's dancing, I discovered, wasn't bad either. It was a fun night, followed by many, many others that summer.

Here are the things that attracted me to Jack: He was a journalism major from Casper, Wyoming. He was warm, friendly, intelligent, articulate, and ambitious. But, though his intention was to follow in his father's newspaper footsteps, he wasn't "locked in" and remained open to other possibilities. He said that what attracted him to me was my independence. I wasn't a sorority girl. I didn't play dumb; and I didn't hide that I had dreams, ideas, and goals of my own.

That summer, I auditioned for a show at the Happy Medium, a popular nightclub on Chicago's busy Rush Street. Gus was doing the choreography and I was delighted to work with him. Jack was in summer school, but when he wasn't in class, he hung out at the theater. He was there so often that theater management asked him if he wanted a job. With no background, he jumped into the position of stage manager for the run of the show. The boy from Wyoming had caught the showbiz bug.

For the next year, Jack and I spent as much time together as our busy schedules allowed. I was a senior, a year ahead of Jack. While I was set to graduate the following June, he was looking for a paid internship between his junior and senior terms. My major was radio and television, and I happened to see a posting on the department bulletin board that the local

CBS affiliate was interviewing for an intern in their news department. I instantly thought of Jack, who responded right away and beat out a dozen more-qualified Northwestern radio and TV majors to get the job. As it turned out, the interviewer was from Montana and the two hit it off. He related to Jack's Wyoming roots and liked his journalism background.

> *"Do such a good job they won't want to let you go."*
> —Jack Missett

As a WBBM intern, Jack resolved that he'd do such a good job that, at the end of his internship, they wouldn't want to let him go. In three months' time, he accomplished his objective and became the youngest employee and lowest man on the ladder. He was a news writer on the nightshift, 11 p.m. to 7 a.m., so he could still attend his senior term classes during the day.

Jack likes to tell the story of what happened next this way:

"They called me in and told me my internship was over, but they wanted me to stay on . . . as a writer, no less. I couldn't wait to tell Judi. I tracked her down, excited to share that, 'I got the job! For sixty-five bucks a week!'

"'Sixty-five bucks?' she said. 'I haven't made less than a hundred dollars a week since I was 14 years old.'

"'Great!' I replied. 'We should get married.'"

Okay, that's not exactly how I remember it. But Jack and I did get married that year, two days before Christmas 1966, at Chicago's St. Nicholas Church. A few close friends and all four of our parents were in attendance, plus Gus and Peg Giordano, who were like godparents to us by then. In honor of my mother's heritage, we had a local Swedish restaurant cater our reception in our very small one-bedroom apartment. There was no honeymoon planned, as both Jack and I had to work the next day.

The following spring, Jack graduated Northwestern and had moved up the ranks at WBBM to become an on-air reporter. Over the next two years, he made his mark with coverage of the Vietnam War, Canadian draft dodgers, the riots at the 1968 Chicago Democratic Convention, and the trial of the Chicago Seven. One special he created, about a "pot party" at Northwestern University, was so controversial that Jack was called to testify before the Federal Communications Commission and the US Congress.

Meanwhile, I was doing more of the things I'd always done in Chicago: auditions, photo and print ad shoots, auto show narrations, industrial theater shows, film work, dinner theater and traveling road shows, and whatever else came my way.

In mid-1968, at Gus's recommendation, Chicago's Gaslight Club, for whom I'd performed many, many road shows, hired me to choreograph their new road show as well as the on-site floor show in their main Speakeasy Room. It was a plum assignment, which I was not about to give up just because I'd recently discovered I was pregnant. In those days, it was not widely accepted that a woman could hold a job *and* be pregnant at the same time. In fact, most pregnant women quietly bowed out of whatever they were doing and retreated into motherhood. Jack and I, and later Gus, discussed this and decided I would continue to work so long as I felt good and remained healthy. I watched my weight and hid my growing baby bump under the long, blousy "hippie" tops that were fashionable at the time. Our daughter, Shanna, arrived on Sunday, December 29. With wispy blond hair and beautiful brown eyes, she was a heart-melting doll. The following day, Jack called the club to explain I wouldn't be in for Monday's rehearsal since I'd just had a baby. "You mean you just *adopted* a baby?" the club manager asked. "No, no . . . she actually gave birth to our first child," Jack told him.

I'd cast and choreographed a great show, and the Gaslight Club Room's 1968 New Year's Eve performance went off without a hitch (albeit without me). Hiding my pregnancy was another one of my personal declarations of independence—this time against an ignorant, patriarchal policy that would eventually change.

Change was in the air all around me. I was now a wife and mother, still working as a professional model and performer, but in need of a new, more flexible path. Looking back now to early 1969, I realize I had collected all the tools I needed to create what would become Jazzercise. I had absorbed my mother's early lessons in entrepreneurship, Joan's creativity in giving an audience what they want, Gus's professional polish of my dancing and choreography, and Jack's example to stay flexible and open to new possibilities. My inner voice assured me . . . I was ready to take the next step.

CHAPTER 2
Listen.
Trust.
Act.

Dancing alone is not a business. Focus on your audience. Make sure that what you're offering matches what they're looking for. Or, The Birth of Jazzercise in three acts.

The three questions I'm asked most often are, where did the idea of Jazzercise come from, how did you turn your passion into a profitable business, and what advice can you offer to those who aspire to follow in your entrepreneurial footsteps?

The first question is the easiest; I answer it in detail in this chapter. The second question is more complicated, layered, and nuanced but, I promise you, all the answers I have are in the pages that follow. Finally, for those of you who are aspiring entrepreneurs, independent business owners, and future CEOs, there is a special section at the end of each chapter just for you. It's called Clef Notes because the clef is the symbol or key to understanding the pitch of notes on a musical staff. It's a bottom-line list of the key lessons learned, important considerations, and specific takeaways you can use from each chapter's subject matter. I hope you'll find these notes useful in surveying my journey as you contemplate yours.

Throughout my childhood and teen years, I had a heart full of passion for dancing and a head full of dreams—so many dreams—but the two that were most important to me were, number one, to perform professionally in the theater and, number two, to make sure I could always take care of myself, support myself, and not depend on anyone else financially. By age 25, I was living my number one dream, having successfully honed my passion into a full-time career as a professional dancer and entertainer. But financial independence? My number two dream was still just that, a dream with no clear path or plan. If you're at that point in your career—ready to take a leap but not sure how, when, or where—perhaps I can help.

SOMETIMES YOU DON'T KNOW WHAT YOU DON'T KNOW UNTIL IT'S STARING YOU IN THE FACE

In the hot, humid summer of 1969, Jack and I joined the local YMCA, mainly to beat the heat in their indoor, air-conditioned swimming pool. Little Shanna took her first tadpole swim class that year, and afterward, while she played with others in the free daycare area, I'd go for a cooling swim myself. One day, two muscle-bound YMCA employees had set up a booth inviting members to "find your fitness level." Curious, I agreed to be weighed and measured, then have my heart rate and blood pressure monitored before and after a few minutes on the treadmill, some basic sit-ups, pull-ups, and jumps. After each test, I noticed that the two young men exchanged puzzled looks as they noted my "score" then asked me to do something else.

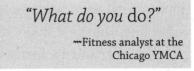

"What do you do?"

—Fitness analyst at the Chicago YMCA

At the end of the tests, which, by the way, were geared toward men not women, one of them declared me "the most physically fit person we've seen!"

"Seriously?" I wondered.

"What do you *do*?" the other one asked.

"I'm a dancer. I dance," I replied.

"That's it? That's *all*?" they asked, clearly surprised.

I must admit that I was surprised too. In 1969, the world of physical fitness with its military-based calisthenics, its treadmill-trudging and weight-lifting workouts (keyword:

work), rarely overlapped with my world of mastering and performing complicated, often challenging jazz dance routines. The idea that dancing could make you certifiably "fit" was a new one to the guys at the Y, and to me.

Since then, scientific studies—most recently in *Frontiers in Aging Neuroscience*—have confirmed that dancing meets or exceeds the amount of energy you burn while running, swimming, or cycling. In addition, in the same way that hiking and trail running engage more joints and muscles than running straight ahead on level ground, dancing's up-and-down and side-to-side movements activate and strengthen many more support muscles and tendons than most traditional exercise options. Plus, the studies report, dancing has been shown to improve "white matter," or connective tissue, in the brain and reduce anxiety and depression.

These things may be widely known now. But back then, this was amazing and gratifying news to me. I remember walking out of the Y that day pondering this new and unique perspective: dancing as a viable way to achieve physical fitness. I couldn't help but wonder at how few people in either the field of fitness or the world of dance realized the connection that I had just serendipitously discovered.

Many entrepreneurs might describe this as an "aha" or "lightbulb" moment, when an innocent curiosity yields a sudden, unexpected clarity. While you can't force a moment like this, you can take advantage when it happens. When you think to yourself, "Hey, this is significant," followed by, "Hmm, what am I supposed to do with this?," put in the time to dive deeper into that gut instinct. My discovery at the Y—

that dancing yields fitness—didn't solve the puzzle, but it was a critical piece in what came next.

ALWAYS CONSIDER YOUR AUDIENCE/CUSTOMERS 2.0

That same summer, Gus asked if I had an interest in teaching a newly organized Saturday morning class called Jazz Dance for Adult Beginners. Quite a few of the women who had signed up were mothers of kids who were taking beginning tap, ballet, or jazz dance classes at Gus's rather large three-story studio. They were there anyway—knitting, reading, sitting around waiting for their kids—so why not dance a little themselves?

> "I'll never be on Broadway. I just wanted to look good for my high school reunion."
>
> ⸺Jazz class dropout

I threw myself into the selection of music, the list of basic moves they'd need to master, some simple choreography, all in line with the "Giordano technique." After our brief warmup and stretching, I did what Gus would do: demonstrate a routine for the group, break down each move by its component parts, direct each student to compare their form to mine in the mirror behind me, then walk around and make individual adjustments.

Unfortunately, over the next few weeks I found myself

with a 90 percent dropout rate. Clearly, I reasoned, there was some sort of disconnect between what I was offering and what my customers wanted. I was bewildered and humbled, and not at all sure what I'd done wrong. The only thing I could think to do was to find the phone numbers of the dropouts, call them up, and ask them why they'd left my class.

In the face of a setback or rejection you need to get to the bottom of why. Do this by asking the people you've disappointed to enlighten you. You don't need to do a fancy survey. Just get up the courage and the gumption to ask them what went wrong. The truth can be difficult to hear, but there's no surer way to avoid making the same mistake twice.

ASK YOUR QUESTIONS, THEN LISTEN, LISTEN, LISTEN

Some of my ex-students were reticent at first, not wanting to hurt my feelings, I suppose. But once I explained I was truly interested in making the class match their expectations— boy, did I get an earful! And I listened carefully to each one:

"I took dance class as a kid and loved it. I was hoping to get that feeling back but didn't."

"Plain and simple, it was too hard for me. I couldn't do it. I just couldn't remember the counts or the steps."

"It seemed more geared to professional status. I'll never be on Broadway. I just want to look good for my high school reunion this fall. Pick up some moves, maybe drop a dress size or two."

"I don't want to be a professional dancer; I just want to look like one."

"I hated seeing all the things I *couldn't* do in the mirror. It was demoralizing."

"Honestly, I thought it would be fun. It wasn't."

Ouch. The truth can hurt but, by clearly identifying your problems, it will also empower you to create a new, more market-based solution. For me, the comment about the mirror, for instance, was particularly helpful. Having grown up in dance studios, I considered the mirror my friend and would never have imagined its negative impact on the unsure or uninitiated. It's important to find out your customers' "pain points" so you can figure the way to lessen or eliminate them.

TRUST THEM, TRUST YOURSELF

I spent time studying the responses of my dropouts. I moped a little, but then I decided to apply some good old common sense to move past feeling rejected to feeling curious. What did I need to do to make the class meet their needs in a more meaningful way? Armed with a clear view of my customers' mindset, I brainstormed an all-new, creative

> *"What if . . . Why not?"*
> ⸺Note to self

class format designed to not only meet but exceed their expectations. I outlined my ideas—many of them radically different from what normally occurred at Giordano Studios—and met with Gus to discuss them.

To his credit, Gus agreed to let me try my new concept, so long as it occurred downstairs in the rarely used back studio.

The flyer I posted announcing a new class called Jazz Dance for Fun and Fitness was meant to directly address my ex-students' complaints, concerns, and needs. And, of course, I personally invited each of my dropouts to give me another try.

The next Saturday, 15 women showed up to "get fit and have fun." The changes I'd made were obvious from the get-go: I stood at the traditional "back" of the studio and turned everyone away from the mirror to face me. The lights—normally bright to focus on small, detailed movements—were adjusted to refocus their attention up front and downplay the mirror in the back. I directed them to follow me through an easy, three-act routine choreographed to a mix of music ranging from jazz classics to popular Top 40 songs. There were no steps to remember, I told them, "just follow me as best you can." After a simple, stretching start, we picked up the beat, gradually moved to a heart-pounding peak, slowed slightly (like an intermission), then closed with a fun finale. All the while, I kept the mood upbeat and provided lots of encouragement.

Did it work? At the end of class, spontaneously, the entire group broke out in applause, for me and for themselves. Without the mirror, they'd engaged the theater of their minds, seeing themselves as active participants in a theatrical performance, rather than passive, nondancing audience members. Once again, I listened closely to their comments after class:

"That was so much fun!"

"Oh, I'm gonna be sore tomorrow."

"Can I bring a friend next time?"

The following week, my class of 15 grew to 30. The week after that, to 60. And, as the initial cohort achieved their objective to have fun and get fit, word spread among the "dance moms" about the new class "for us." I was besieged by offers to add class times.

As had happened to me, very few new products or services hit the mark perfectly the first time. But if you see that failure as an opportunity to listen and learn what your audience/customers *really* want, and adjust and act accordingly, it can quickly become a win-win.

HOW JAZZERCISE GOT ITS NAME

Speaking of listening to your customers, it would be several years before the name of what I was doing became Jazzercise. As with my earlier student survey of what the class should be—today they'd call it "crowd-sourcing"—the idea sprang from listening to my students' insights.

I was living in Southern California by then, and a student in my class at the La Jolla YMCA asked, "What do you call what we're doing?"

> *"You ought to call this Jazzercise."*
>
> ⸺A student in La Jolla, California

"Well, the name of the class is Jazz Dance for Fun and Fitness," I answered.

She knit her brows in thought. "You know, we're doing

lots of jazzy dance moves, but we're also exercising—I think you ought to call this Jazzercise." Immediately, her classmates chimed in, "Hey, that sounds good!" "Kinda catchy." "You should!"

When I surveyed my other classes, they unanimously agreed. One student, Margaret Stanton, even volunteered, "My husband's an attorney. I work in his office and can help you file the paperwork to trademark it."

It can be easy to get caught up in the mindset that you "know all" when it comes to your business—but to do so is a mistake. Your best customers want you to succeed. If you make them feel seen and heard, they can be a terrific source of ideas, insight, and direction. Listen to them and make the changes they need.

A CRUCIAL AWAKENING FOR ME: PASSION PLUS PURPOSE MEANS BUSINESS

At just three years old, in my first dance class, I discovered what would become my lifelong *passion*. Throughout my childhood, teens, college years, and early twenties, I lived to dance and, through very hard work, created a successful career as a pro-

> "Purpose is the reason you journey. Passion is the fire that lights the way."
> ⸺Author unknown

fessional jazz dancer, moving from one theatrical or corporate dance show to the next. Among dancers, the term is *professional gypsy*. It was a tremendously fulfilling career, but it was *never* a business that could be grown, franchised, or scaled globally.

At 25 years old, teaching my first Jazz Dance for Fun and Fitness class, I discovered my greater *purpose*. To do so, I had to shift the focus off myself, my abilities, and my accomplishments and onto others. I had to learn how to use my unique combination of skills and insights to help them achieve their goals of fun, fitness, and, ultimately, a healthier, happier life. Looking back at that shift of focus—that aha moment at the intersection of passion *and* purpose, of seeing clearly the way that my skills could make a meaningfully contribution to the well-being of others—this was the true genesis of what would eventually become Jazzercise.

I call this awakening crucial because I'm approached all the time by others looking for advice to turn their passion into a profitable business. Without a greater purpose, I'm not sure it's possible. Whatever your passion, you can have a very fine career pursuing it. If, however, you aspire to build a business, you must find a way to use your passion to serve and significantly improve the lives of others.

Let me give you two more examples. Bill Gates has said on many occasions, his passion, his life's love was creating software. With that alone, he could have had an extremely successful career as an elite designer. However, Microsoft sprang from the intersection of Bill's passion for software *and* his greater purpose: to make personal computing available to everyone. Similarly, from a very early age Joy Mangano had a passion for problem solving. Most notably, as a single working mother of three, she grew frustrated with the common household mop and so invented the self-wringing Miracle

Mop. Her business, Ingenious Designs, was born at the juncture of her inventive creativity *and* her greater purpose to address the needs of the millions of floor moppers who hated putting their hands in dirty mop water as much as she did.

In both these examples, and in mine, the overriding goal was never simply to make money or turn a profit. It was, instead, to apply our personal skills to help, to serve, to benefit others. Passion *plus* purpose means business. Do it right and the money will follow.

∿

Meanwhile, back at Giordano Studios, Chicago, 1969 . . .

Gus was delighted by the response we were receiving to Jazz Dance for Fun and Fitness. But, as I would soon learn, there were many others who were not.

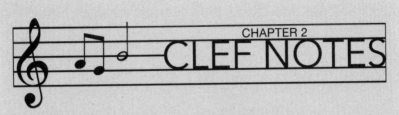

CHAPTER 2
CLEF NOTES

♪ Whatever your passion, think of it as the bass beat for everything you do, the different drum that you hear more clearly than anything else.

♪ Turning your passion into a profession may take years of practice, hard work, and strong mentoring to achieve the level of mastery. Professional secret here, however: when you're doing what you love, it may not seem like work at all.

♪ Turning your profession into a profitable business requires discovering and defining your larger purpose. How can you use your unique perspective, abilities, and offering to enhance or improve the lives of many others? Your answer to this question is crucial to creating and building a business of any size.

♪ As you begin to define and explore your business concept, you will experience trial and error. At Jazzercise, we know our customers vote with their feet. If they're not showing up, something is wrong. View this as an opportunity to ask questions and to listen and learn from your audience/customers. Trust their input. Then trust your own ability to reassess, reimagine, and redesign something new, more acceptable, and exciting.

♪ If that doesn't work, persevere. Reconnect to your passion, your own personal beat. Keep listening, keep trusting, and, most important, keep trying. The answer is out there waiting for you.

CHAPTER 3

Expect Resistance. Do It Anyway.

There will be skeptics and cynics. As Taylor Swift says, "Shake it off!" Stand up for yourself and what you believe.

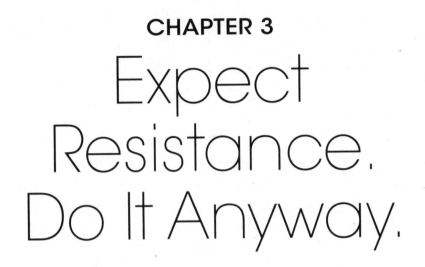

SOME PEOPLE JUST WON'T GET IT

The first year I was teaching my new class was a heady time. While I continued to dance, choreograph, and pick up modeling and performing gigs, Jack was getting more and more airtime as a TV reporter for the local CBS affiliate; and two-year-old Shanna, who had adopted Gus and Peg Giordano as her local grandparents, was our communal delight.

With 60 students, Saturday morning's Jazz Dance for Fun and Fitness was fully enrolled with a bulging waitlist to get in. My students arrived eager and excited to begin. They were having

> *"You're bastardizing the art form!"*
> —A fellow jazz dancer

fun and, week by week, getting fit. More important, I could see them taking ownership of their bodies in new ways: postures were improving, stances more confident, and movements smoother and more comfortably sexy. They weren't becoming dancers, per se—certainly not elite Giordano jazz dancers, known for precise and highly refined techniques— but they were women discovering, many for the first time, the joy of fully embracing physical movement to music, absorbing the rhythm, feeling the beat, which is the heart of dance.

Around the larger studio, the "dance moms" were calling it "our class" while, among my fellow dancers and instructors, it had become "Judi's thing." It wasn't long before I could see my colleagues' heads popping around the corner, brows furrowed, lips bit, wondering what all the buzz was about. I suppose I could have, and maybe should have, expected them to be skeptical. At first, I was quietly asked, "What's your thinking here?" Another, in a mix of horror and concern, demanded, "What are you doing?" Most memorable was the one—whom I considered a friend, by the way—who fumed, "You're bastardizing the art form!" followed by "Has Gus seen *this*?"

Their almost unanimous outrage reminded me of President John Kennedy's quote, "Change is the law of life. And those who look only to the past or present are certain to miss the future." My fellow instructors were classicists. They'd worked hard to rise to their elite levels. I understood their concerns, but I also felt they were being snobs. Why shouldn't the joy and benefits of jazz dance, in a simplified form, be available to everyone?

Fortunately, Gus agreed with me. "It's really quite an innovative thing you're doing, Judi. You're not training dancers, but you are creating an appreciative audience for what we do," he said. "Plus, they're obviously having fun and feeling good. Where's the harm in that?"

For the next three years, until Jack and I left Chicago, my hybridized Jazz Dance for Fun and Fitness class was among the most popular and predictably full of any at Giordano Studios, despite the consternation of the staff purists.

Whenever you start a new business, change directions, or push back against the norm, you can expect your own set of resisters. Colleagues who were once patting you on the back are suddenly talking behind your back. It hurts, and it can be hard to ignore their doubts and move forward with confidence and clarity. Stick with what's driving you to change: your passion, your insights, your ability to innovate and connect with your customers. Realize that the dissenters may lack the awareness to see what you see or the courage to do what you're doing. Stay focused and keep moving toward your future.

FAMILY RESISTANCE CAN
BE CHALLENGING

In the middle of a blizzard, late fall 1971, Jack and I sat at the kitchen table of our suburban Chicago townhouse tak-ing stock. WBBM-TV had recently hired a new, fiercely competitive news director to take the station in a differ-ent direction, harder edged,

> *"California dreamin', on such a winter's day . . ."*
> ---The Mamas and the Papas

in-studio, and driven by the adage "if it bleeds, it leads." Jack, who'd gained a reputation for his off-site human-interest sto-ries, was one of 40 CBS staffers laid off in the transition, just before Halloween.

We were in our late twenties and had been working non-stop since high school. We had some savings, we had Jack's layoff package, which included CBS stock, and we had, in front of us, receipts for the nine different trips we'd taken to California that year to visit Jack's brothers in coastal Ocean-side north of San Diego.

"You know, if there was ever a good time for us to make a move," Jack said, "it's probably now." I agreed.

Saying good-bye to our friends and jazz family was hard. I'd been a wide-eyed, 18-year-old college freshman when I arrived, up for anything; and now I was a 27-year-old wife, mother, and seasoned professional, with skills, experience, and a head full of big ideas. "Peg and I were about your age when we left New York for Chicago. It was a scary move for us but, obviously," Gus said, with the sweep of his hand taking in the sunny upstairs studio, the three-story building that was a mecca to jazz dancers from around the world, "it all worked out just fine."

"Shoulders back, chin up, Judi," Peg added. "If we come across any work that suits you, we'll send it your way." Dear Peg and Gus would remain helpful, trusted friends and mentors for the rest of their lives.

Within weeks, we'd packed up Shanna and our lives in Chicago and headed southwest, bound for Southern California. Our first stop was for Thanksgiving with my conservative parents in Red Oak, Iowa. In the kitchen, my practical mother asked, "Are there any dance studios, any jazz companies, any potential places for you to work in North San Diego County?"

I withheld the real answers (which were *no*, *no*, and *I don't know*) and stayed positive, replying simply, "I hope so."

In the dining room, my father grilled Jack, then pronounced us both "long on dreams, short on details."

Although neither of my parents were exactly supportive, I reminded them both that Jack and I had been raised with strong values and a hard work ethic, which would serve us well, no matter what we faced in California. If you don't believe in yourself, who will?

Our next stop, pre-Christmas, was with Jack's parents in Casper, Wyoming. Jack's dad was the publisher of the *Casper Star Tribune*. All three of Jack's older brothers had followed their father into the newspaper business and were involved in Oceanside's *North County Times*.

"So, Jack," his dad asked, "does this mean you're finally going to put your degree in journalism to good use?"

To Jack's credit, he answered truthfully. "I don't know,

Dad. I'm kind of burnt out on the news right now. Maybe I'll try my hand at a novel, or a screenplay."

Pause here to imagine the lifelong newsman's barely suppressed eyeroll. Jack's father, with a reporter's bias against fiction, was less than impressed.

Just after Christmas, we resumed our journey west, over the snow-capped Rockies, across the beautiful-in-winter California desert, to our new year and new life in coastal Oceanside. We knew our hardworking parents were concerned about us. It was only natural, considering who they were. But we were emboldened by our faith in each other and our individual selves that somehow, despite their fears, we'd find a way to make California work for us. It felt like the right place to be and the perfect time to be there.

In my mind, a leap of faith is just that. You can always choose to listen to the naysayers, step away from change, and live with regret the rest of your life. Or (and this is my preference) you can choose to ignore the critics, take the chance, make the leap, and trust yourself to deal with what comes. When your leap of faith is fueled by your passion and sense of purpose, it's easier to take the risk and not let others change your mind.

MY NOT-SO-GOLDEN OPPORTUNITY AT THE GOLDEN DOOR

What came over the next two years after our move to California was a wide variety of opportunities, including a six-month sojourn in Aspen, Colorado; several theatrical and corporate gigs in Los Angeles, Chicago, and Aspen; and, whenever possible, further refinement of my Jazz Dance for Fun and Fitness classes in Oceanside and La Jolla.

> *"You're fired!"*
> ⸺Deborah Szekely, owner of the world-renowned Golden Door spa

In the spring of 1974, with our cash reserves running low, I reluctantly accepted a part-time job (my first-ever punch-the-clock position) with Deborah Szekely at the renowned Golden Door spa in Escondido, half an hour east of Oceanside. In any given week, our very exclusive clientele could include celebrities, wealthy socialites, businesswomen, and the wives of assorted millionaires.

My wide-ranging job was to teach dance and exercise classes, lead water aerobics in the pool, go on outdoor hikes on the surrounding 330 acres of mountain trails, and lead indoor strength or weight-training sessions in the gym. Although Jack and I joked that it was my "golden opportunity," it often involved long days of hard work (some guests made it a lot harder than others) for steady income plus tips. Because it was part-time, I also continued to teach evening classes in La Jolla and Oceanside and accept small local dancing and choreography gigs.

That fall, in fact, I had eagerly jumped at the chance to choreograph and perform entertainment for the lavish annual charity gala of the Soroptimist Club of upscale La Jolla. For weeks, I had scheduled everything to do with the show— casting, rehearsals, costume fittings—around my Golden Door shifts to avoid any conflict. Unfortunately, however, the show itself was on a Friday night, which was also a Golden Door workday for me. That afternoon, sensing my stress over the traffic between Escondido and La Jolla and my ability to get there on time to direct and perform the show, a kind coworker encouraged me to take off 20 minutes early. "Deborah's out of town; I'll cover for you," she said. I admit I bolted out of there and drove like a madwoman west to La Jolla. The show that night could not have gone better. We received several standing ovations and the Soroptimists made a lot of money. It was a win-win, I thought. Until I received the call the following day that Deborah wanted to see me in her office first thing Monday morning.

Apparently, Deborah had called the spa just before five o'clock and asked to speak with me. My coworker had tried and failed to put her off. That Monday, in no uncertain terms, Deborah explained that, even though my position was part-time, "I like my people to be exclusive, and I expect them to adhere to the rules. You've done a great job, but nobody gets special treatment other than our guests. Please pick up your things and leave." And just like that, six weeks before Christmas, I was out of my only real job.

The last thing Deborah said to me, as she showed me the suddenly-not-so-golden door, was, "Someday, you'll thank me for this." One day years later, I did.

I'm sharing this story because it demonstrates a negative turning point—we all experience them—that would, as Deborah predicted, eventually turn into a positive. Initially, though, the words "You're fired!" hit me like an emotional body blow. I'd made what seemed to me a small mistake with immediate and, at the time, huge consequences. I was wrong, no doubt about it, and I felt terrible. In fairness to Deborah, I had received several requests to teach more of my classes in Oceanside and La Jolla and planned to quit the Golden Door the first of the year. She'd simply pushed up the timeline by two months. But as I drove home to our little rental house in Vista and flung myself into Jack's arms with the news, all I could think was "There goes Christmas!" because money was so tight.

"We'll get through this," Jack promised. The next day he left in the morning and came back that afternoon with three jobs. By day, he worked at East San Diego's Claremont Mesa Shopping Centre as a part-time Santa and at Two Guys Discount Electronics as a part-time shelf stacker. By night, he covered the graveyard shift at Oceanside's Scandia Bakery, arriving home just after 5 a.m. with fresh, warm baked goods for breakfast.

Jack was my support person, my team. When the going gets tough, and it inevitably will, you need someone to talk to or lean on. It can be isolating and difficult to go it alone. All the negative feelings—anger, guilt, fear, a bit of panic over lost income—can seem overwhelming. There's no shame in asking for help to consciously recast your situation in a more positive light. When analyzing a difficult and challenging situation, two heads or more are always better and more productive than one.

Christmas was lean that year. We ate a lot of free bread and pastries, and most of our gifts were homemade. While Jack worked his three jobs, I worked the phone, calling my contacts in Oceanside and La Jolla. Of course, it was the absolute worst time of year to add any classes. Nevertheless, I was able to add a few new morning classes, even though most people were focused on their holiday festivities, not signing up for fitness. Then, just before New Year's, a seed sown at the Soroptimist gala the Friday before I got fired bore fruit. A man who had attended the gala called, saying he wanted to introduce me to his friend John Cates, who ran community fitness programs at the University of California in San Diego, and also to John Sonnhalter, head of Parks and Recreation in the city of Carlsbad.

Further, the big show on Broadway that season was *A Chorus Line*. It won both the Pulitzer Prize and the Tony Award for Best Musical and, more important for me, heightened public interest in jazz dancing.

That January, thanks to my dogged pursuit of old and new contacts, my late afternoons, evenings, and weekends were filled with classes, and I was burning up the 5 Freeway driving between my commitments in La Jolla, Encinitas, and Oceanside, and a new extensive schedule at Carlsbad Parks and Rec.

Although I don't believe the old saying "time heals all wounds" is exactly true, I do think that time can and often does yield a necessary change in your perspective. When you are deep in the muck on your hardest days, hang in there, stay focused on the positive, and continue to pursue your mission. Stay creative and do what you have to do. Eventually, your nonstop efforts will produce results—even if it doesn't feel like it right now.

It's also worth noting that painful experiences, like getting fired as an employee, can inform your policy-making when you're the boss. Today, at Jazzercise, any employee separation, voluntary or involuntary (after three written warnings), is handled with the utmost kindness, compassion, and respect—as it should be.

STAND UP FOR YOURSELF AND WHAT YOU KNOW IS RIGHT

One of the great joys of doing what you love for a living is that you often work harder than you realize because it doesn't really feel like work at all. By late that spring, even I was surprised that the monthly fee due to me for my classes in Carlsbad had jumped to

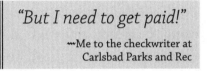

"But I need to get paid!"

⸺Me to the checkwriter at Carlsbad Parks and Rec

more than $1,000. When I stopped by the office to pick up my check, the receptionist told me there was "some sort of a problem" and I needed to speak with "the guy who writes the checks" personally.

I walked in and was asked, point-blank, "How am I supposed to pay you this much?"

"I don't understand," I replied. "It's all according to our contract."

"I need approval from the city council to write a check this large, which is, by the way, significantly more than we pay any of our other Parks and Rec instructors."

"Because," I stammered, "I'm teaching more classes than they are!"

"That may be true, but a check this size . . . well, it's *embarrassing* for me to write a check this big to—"

The words "a woman," maybe even "a little exercise girl like you," hung in the air between us, unspoken. It was 1975, only one year after the Senate had passed the Equal Credit Opportunity Act, making it illegal to financially discriminate against someone based on their gender, race, religion, or national origin, and change was slow.

"But I need to get paid!"

"Not today. I'll have to submit this and get back to you."

I walked away stunned. I'd overcome a lot of challenges in Carlsbad—securing rooms big enough for my classes at times convenient for me and my customers' schedules, arranging child care for those who needed it—but not getting paid for work I'd already done was a new and painful one. As every entrepreneur knows, cash flow is the oxygen that keeps your business afloat. The following week, the week after that, and the week after that, I was given the bureaucratic brush-off. "Not yet, we're working on it," I was told. By the fourth week, I was owed more than $2,000! And I was *mad*.

I arrived at the office with my latest invoice in hand, as well as a copy of my previous month's invoice clearly marked PAST DUE. When the receptionist shook her head to say "nothing yet," I demanded to see "the guy who writes the checks" again.

Jack and I had discussed this, even rehearsed it. I sat down and very calmly explained, "I have a contract that hasn't been paid for two months now. I earned the money, and I deserve to be paid. I'm not sure that you are aware, but my brother-in-law is the publisher of the *North County Times* newspaper, and another brother-in-law is its editor. If you do not pay me by four o'clock this afternoon, I'm heading straight to their offices in Oceanside to tell them that Carlsbad Parks and Rec is withholding payment from a legitimate vendor. I'll be back for my check," I said, rising to go, "at four o'clock." Or, at least that's what I planned.

That afternoon, I walked in at exactly four and noted the door to his office was closed.

"Is he here?" I asked the receptionist.

"No, he left," she said.

Boy, was I angry! I turned to go, fuming, then stopped myself. Turning back, I asked, "Do you have something for me?"

"Oh, yes," she answered and handed me an envelope with my check in it.

~~~

Although I was given what I had hoped for, that experience taught me something: the problem wasn't this man's unwillingness to write the check (although his reluctance to give money to a woman who ran a business he didn't understand was an issue too); it was his bureaucratic inability to do so easily. How could I work around that? I wondered.

I also discovered an additional issue when I was told that Parks and Rec only permitted monthly class registrations on a certain day each month and, as a result, my students were lining up as early as 5 a.m. on the signup day to make sure they got into my classes. Another bureaucratic knot that needed untangling.

In my experience, bureaucracies can get stuck in the "we've always done it this way" trap. The mindset is maddening, especially to a creative entrepreneur. The secret to dealing with them is to see things from their perspective, figure out their needs and challenges, and offer an alternative that solves or simplifies their problems as well as yours.

Determined to move forward, I asked for another meeting with Mr. Check Writer to propose a mutually beneficial solution. "Instead of you dealing with the 5 a.m. crush of my students signing up here each month, as well as the paperwork involved in individual collections, what if I handle sign-ups in class, collect payments from them, retain my contracted 90 percent share, and write Parks and Rec a check for your 10 percent share?" When I sensed a bit of interest on his part, I continued, "This would not only simplify your life, it would ease my students' stress over signing up and resolve my cash flow issue. Win-win-win all around!" Reflecting on how my plan would benefit *him*, he agreed.

Often, in the face of someone openly resisting you, the problem is not what it seems and can be more easily resolved than you think. This is something I discuss further in Chapter 7, "Hard Yeses, Flexible Nos, and the Magical Power of *Why Not?*"

CHAPTER 3
CLEF NOTES

♪ Once you've married your passion to a greater purpose, received confirmation from your customers, and absolutely clarified the mission of your business, anchor it internally with all the steely courage and iron-clad conviction you can muster. You'll need to because . . .

♪ You will encounter resistance from a variety of sources: envious colleagues, obtuse friends, or even concerned and caring family members. And you'll find, soon enough, you can't buy or borrow self-confidence. You must draw it yourself from your own bone-deep belief in what you're doing. In the earliest days of your business, you'll be visiting that well often.

♪ Not all resistance will be verbal. It can also show up in unreturned phone calls, untrusting vendors, or a lost job. Getting fired really fired me up to refocus with renewed energy on my mission. It's often hard to remember that in every exit or ending lies the seed of a new beginning. Hang in there, search for the positive, and keep moving forward.

♪ Find your support person or team. It doesn't take a village. Often, just one individual or a small group of friends who believe in you and will listen with support instead of judgment will do.

♪ There will come a time when you and you alone must stand up for yourself and what you know is right. Take time to let go of your anger, upset, and frustration, and clearly consider the situation from both sides. Look for a mutually beneficial solution, and confidently propose a win-win alternative. Be clear in advance what you need out of the negotiation, and always leave the other person room to do the right thing. Most people will. If not, you may have to walk away, but with your dignity intact.

PART TWO

MAINTAIN YOUR RHYTHM THROUGH GROWTH AND CHANGE

Life is a lot like jazz . . . it's best when you improvise.
—George Gershwin

To keep creating you have to be about change.
—Miles Davis

CHAPTER 4

Watch for Cues, Signs, and Signals

In dance, there's a term—musicality—which means the ability to connect your body with the rhythm, melody, and mood of a song. You must be aware of the present moment while at the same time you're listening for the cue to where you need to go next. I believe that in business and in life, the process is the same: Awareness. Acceptance. Action.

Judi

Regardless of where you are in the life span of your business, it is a living, growing thing that constantly provides you with cues about its environment, market, products, customers, vendors, employees, or management. As its leader, you are responsible for anticipating and interpreting the important signals your business sends you concerning its needs, difficulties, or challenges.

Read any entrepreneur's story and you'll see that either spotting a sign correctly or missing an important signal altogether can be the difference between sweet success and a painful disaster. I've had my share of both. Some signs stop you in your tracks and demand immediate path-altering decision-making. Others are subtler but no less critical. The key, I believe, is to reframe the challenge to be proactive, instead of simply reactive.

THE CUE THAT I NEEDED TO LET GO OF SOLE CONTROL

By 1977, my schedule was jam-packed with 25 classes per week, plus weekend workshops and publicity demos. Each class generally involved 50 to 60 students who followed my on-stage physical moves and vocal instructions and encouragements called out to them over the music. By the end of most weeks, my

> *"You have nodules on your vocal chords, due to overuse. . . . You're at risk of losing your voice entirely."*
> —My voice specialist

voice was a bit hoarse. But as the year wore on, my voice became more and more strained, leaving me most weekends with little more than a whisper.

I went to our family doctor hoping he'd suggest some sort of restorative spray or lozenges. Instead, he referred me to an ear, nose, and throat doctor, who referred me to an "otolaryngologist," or voice specialist.

After examining my vocal chords, the specialist asked, "What do you do exactly?" When I explained, he said, "Well, no wonder!"

"You have nodules and calluses on your vocal chords, due to overuse," he said. "We could operate and remove them, but given your schedule, they'd most likely come back. My immediate prescription is complete silence, not even a whisper, for five days. Write notes. Do *not* talk. We'll see if it helps. Further, you must either quit teaching so many classes or find someone to help you. Otherwise, you're at risk of losing your voice entirely." *That* got my attention!

I admit my husband, Jack, and others had suggested the idea that I train other instructors to take on some of my classes and field the phone calls requesting new classes in other areas; but I was concerned that wouldn't work. I thought that Jazzercise was just me and my personality and the way I moved. I was convinced that, unless I could be cloned, the experience couldn't be replicated. Of course, my ego was in play as well. Who wants to think they're easily replaced? Losing my voice was a sign, however, that perhaps I needed to let go of sole control.

Hesitantly, I approached five of my most experienced students, who'd already mastered my most recent routines, with handwritten notes asking if they would consider taking over my classes while I recuperated. Each one said yes. And, truly, one of the happiest days of my life was when I received a call from a longtime student saying, "Nikki [Miller] just finished teaching our class and she was great, we loved it. She was different than you are, but it was really terrific!" Hanging up, my thought was, "Hallelujah! Now we can begin to share this with a lot more people."

Decades later, I see clearly that losing my voice helped me gain the perspective that was critical to growing Jazzercise from a series of local classes to a worldwide dance fitness organization. It's a common entrepreneurial problem—the idea that you and you alone can do what needs to be done. The solution is often as simple as checking your ego and realizing that, though others may do things differently, they're perfectly capable of getting the job done.

While your sign that it's time to let go of sole control may not be as dramatic as mine, if you're growing, you're going to have to face the fact that you are not superhuman. The bigger your business, the heavier the burden on your body, mind, spirit, relationships, and overall life. Watch for the inevitable stress point signaling that a second pair of capable hands (or more) is needed to free you to do bigger and better things— and don't be scared of that call. It just means your business is growing!

TWO SIGNS IT WAS TIME TO EMBRACE EMERGING TECHNOLOGIES

Training others to do what you've been doing single-handedly for years can be daunting. My first step was to examine the many hats I was wearing and decide which could be worn by others. At the time, I was booking and managing all my own classes; choreographing new routines to classic, standard, and Top 40 songs; and approaching each of my 25 weekly classes as a fun and fitness-producing 55-minute group performance. My inclination was to train instructors in the performance aspects of presenting a Jazzercise class and let them independently book and manage their own classes. Meanwhile, in exchange for a small percentage of their gross income, I would permit them to use the Jazzercise name and regularly provide newly choreographed dance routines to a creative mix of popular music. (A core strength of Jazzercise, even today, is our constant innovation and evolution of new dance moves and fitness techniques to new songs and formats.) As an entrepreneur, you're wearing many more hats than you realize. I suggest making a list of everything you're doing on a regular basis. Which roles do you do best? Which could be handled by others or outsourced? Once you answer

> *"Do you mind if we videotape the new routines? It will be so much easier to review when we get home."*
>
> —Two Jazzercise instructors from 29 Palms, California

those questions, figure out how to delegate them so you can spend your time doing what you do best.

After a few weekend workshops, my first five instructors were empowered to start their own businesses, just as I had, by borrowing or renting spaces, posting flyers, signing up students, and teaching Jazzercise. Before long, another five students approached me for training, rounding out the First Ten. Within several months, we'd grown to 30 "certified Jazzercise instructors" throughout Southern California.

Having additional teachers enabled me to cut my own class schedule in half, to 12 a week; devote more time to choreographing new routines; and provide support for our rapidly growing team. One immediate challenge was translating my new routines into written choreographic notes. I'd always handwritten notes to myself but—another sign—typing was not my forte! When I asked in class if anyone would like to earn a little something by typing my notes, once again Margaret Stanton, who'd helped me file trademark papers, volunteered. It wasn't long before Margaret became our first full-time employee and eventually chief operating officer. What a relief to have someone to lean on whose strengths were different and complementary to mine.

At critically important weekend teacher workshops, we'd meet to discuss any issues, share tips, learn new routines, and permit aspiring teachers to "try out" by leading the group through a routine they felt they'd mastered. Every new routine was accompanied by carefully typed choreographic notes, a practice we continue to this day. One weekend, however, two instructors, Karen Brodie and Marsha Cole from 29 Palms, near Palm Springs, showed up with a large video camera and tripod. Marsha, I learned, was married to a high school principal, who had allowed them to borrow the school's expensive equipment, which was not then available for home use.

"Do you mind if we videotape the new routines?" they asked. "It will be so much easier to review when we get home."

Of course I said yes, with the certainty that this was a fantastic idea. Over the next few months, while Karen and Marsha continued to tape our sessions, I peppered Jack—who'd been a TV reporter, remember—with questions: "How much do these new video cameras cost? Where can we buy one? What else would we need?" A major concern was, "If we buy a camera and make the tapes, can our instructors afford a home videocassette recorder to play them back?"

The following weekend, Jack and I drove down to a store in Clairemont Mesa, the area of San Diego adjacent to a couple of TV stations. After several deep breaths, we settled on a Panasonic video camera (a whopping $1,400), plus two top-loading VCRs ($1,000 each), and several dozen blank VHS tapes ($20 apiece). It was a large up-front check for me, but an investment we were certain would pay off in the end.

That year, 1977, was the first year VHS technology was available in the United States. As time passed, the prices for cameras, VCRs, and tapes came down significantly. A good thing, too, because by 1979 we'd grown to 100 instructors and needed 24 VCRs to make copies for everyone every six weeks. Poor Jack, who had volunteered to handle the duping, labeling, and shipping of tapes, lived with a stopwatch around his neck tracking when it was time to reload the multiple VCRs with blank cassettes.

Jack also took on taping my new routines, first in the

backyard where our dog, Blackie, made several unscripted cameo appearances, and eventually in our own JMTV studios with three professional JVC studio cameras, 100 VCR decks, plus two employees to take on the constant duping work. Today, in a nod to the technology we now use, it's called JM DigitalWorks.

When you're a budding entrepreneur, it can be expensive to embrace constantly evolving technology. But the cost of not embracing it can be even higher. Without our early and first use of videotaped (and now live-streamed) training, we could never have grown as fast and gone as far as we have.

In 1979, I noticed something odd at our Saturday morning teacher workshops. Even with the cutback in my class schedule, my voice was still hoarse by the end of the week. And I wasn't the only one. We all had strained and raspy voices from projecting over the music.

> *"Still getting hoarse? Why don't you use a microphone?"*
> ⸺My otolaryngologist, again

When I returned to my voice specialist, his question was, "Still getting hoarse? Why don't you use a microphone?" And this sent me off on another technological quest. This time, I was looking for the perfect microphone to use while teaching a high-energy dance fitness class.

Unfortunately, the technology we needed—a small, lightweight, wireless and sweat-resistant mic—didn't exist, and it wouldn't for many years. So, we began experimenting with available options. After trying many different solutions, from duct tape to necklaces to vertical stands, we became one of the first to try a new, lighter-weight Audio Technica mic. In the 1980s, we tested and adopted the first wireless lapel mics by Nady and Shure, and in the 1990s, when lightweight wireless headset mics became available (originally developed by NASA), we pioneered their use in the fitness industry. We were always open to experimentation and this is something you must embrace as well. You'll never know if something could work or spark a new idea unless you try.

When you're an entrepreneur, necessity is indeed the mother of invention. The same creativity you use in developing your product and business will serve you well in solving the challenges that inevitably pop up in other areas. Define the need, assess your options, experiment, and when all else fails, improvise.

HOW ONE GOOD THING CAN SIGNAL ANOTHER

In August of 1979, I was invited to perform a short demonstration of Jazzercise on Dinah Shore's popular TV show. It was to be my first national television appearance and we really spread the word so everyone we knew—instructors, students, friends, and family—would watch.

A few days before the show, I had a last-minute brainstorm and visited my artistic friend Connie Williams to ask if there was any

> *"Where can I get one of those Jazzercise leotards that Judi wore on 'The Dinah Shore Show'?"*
>
> ---Jazzercise instructors and students nationwide

way we could silk-screen the word *Jazzercise* across the front of the red leotard I planned to wear. When Connie said yes, I added that it needed to be as big as possible, so viewers at home could read it.

Connie, God bless her, really came through. She not only put the word in a jazzy typeface with stars dotting the *j* and *i*—an instant logo—but she also somehow got it silk-screened in white across the red, so it really popped. I couldn't have been happier. I felt great wearing it, and nobody who saw the show could miss the name Jazzercise.

The point of this story is that one good thing (e.g., my appearance on Dinah's show) often signals it is time for another (this time, merchandising), *if* you pay attention to the signs.

Quite unexpectedly, after the show aired, we were besieged by instructor and customer requests. "Where can I get one of those Jazzercise leotards like Judi wore on 'The Dinah Shore Show'?" "Does it come in other colors?" "Which ones?" "What else is available?"

Out of the blue, we discovered there was an interest and an easily accessible audience for our own leotards. For a while Connie and I pooled our money to buy and silk-screen more leotards. Eventually, the demand grew so great that Margaret brought in Cindy Luxton and later Kristie Viveiros to create and manage Jazzertogs, an accidentally created division of the company, which has since grown into Jazzercise Apparel. Now led by Joan Marie Wallace, Jazzercise Apparel designs, produces, and sells brand-name and licensed clothing and accessories to the tune of $5.8 million per year.

Sometimes you work really hard to develop a great business concept and an additional opportunity falls right in your lap because of the first one. Our serendipitous apparel division not only helped establish our brand visually and provided an additional revenue source, but it also broadened our presence within our target markets, as happy and fit customers and instructors proudly sported their branded apparel around their towns. That was an outcome we didn't expect or anticipate. Keep your eyes open for ways one success can open the door to another and be willing to adapt accordingly.

THE MESSAGE NO ENTREPRENEUR WANTS TO HEAR

By 1982, we had more than 1,000 certified instructors teaching Jazzercise classes in almost every state plus a few foreign countries. We'd recently heard that our first Jazzercise record album had gone gold (i.e., sold more than 25,000 copies) and the book *Jazzercise: A Fun Way to Fitness* was a bestseller in its fourth printing. In addition, I was pregnant with Brendan, our second child. By all accounts, life was good.

Then I received word that our company attorney, Stan Green, and our accountant, Leonard Pariser, both in Beverly Hills, needed to schedule an urgent conference call. This was a double red flag; I'd always met with either Stan or Leonard separately, and they had never jointly requested an *urgent* call.

Stan, who was not one to mince words, led off with,

> *"What you're doing is illegal."*
>
> ⸻Company attorney Stanley H. Green and CPA Leonard Pariser

"Sorry to be the bearer of bad news, Judi, but what you're doing is illegal."

"The problem," Leonard added, "is that your relationship with your instructors does not meet the Internal Revenue Service's strict definition for independent contractors."

"Bottom line," Stan said, "you have a very hard choice to make. Either turn them all into Jazzercise employees or convert them all to franchisees."

Every entrepreneur faces major, gut-wrenching turning points. This was mine. Just like the leap of faith required to get into business in the first place, this required a leap into the hard facts of what I was facing, and a very tough choice that would significantly impact the lives and futures of everyone involved in the company.

Unfortunately, my advisors were split. Accountant Leonard favored the employee option and attorney Stan was on the side of franchising.

As I considered both options, the faces of all the women who had started as students and were now off creating their own Jazzercise success in other states flashed through my mind: Jeri Sipe in Ohio, DeeDee Kovacevich in New Mexico, Peggy Leinenkugel in Wisconsin, among many others. All were powerful, enthusiastic women possessed of the same entrepreneurial passion and purpose that I was. Would they want to become employees? Would I want to be their boss? Wasn't Jazzercise, at its heart, as much about empowering our instructors to be independent businesswomen as it was about encouraging our students to discover the joy and fun of a healthier life and more confident self?

In the end, I chose the franchise option, with a twist.

Going against the industry norm, which generally charged a high buy-in fee (upwards of $25,000) and a lower 3 percent to 10 percent royalty rate, we did the opposite—enabling an instructor to become a Jazzercise franchisee for only $500, plus 20 percent of their monthly gross receipts minus rent. Some called our formula cockeyed, but it worked for us and for our franchisees. In 1983, a successful Jazzercise franchise (and most were very successful) could easily provide the owner with a net annual income of $75,000. That's the equivalent, in today's dollars, of $187,495 per year.

Converting our instructors into franchisees was a tough choice, but it was undeniably the right one. By 1985, Jazzercise was named the number two bestselling franchise in the country, second only to Domino's Pizza. When faced with a gut-wrenching decision, in business and in life, my advice is always "gut, head, heart." Check your gut, your inner voice; engage your brain; and proceed with heart.

CROSSED SIGNALS FROM HIGH-PRICED CONSULTANTS

In the early years of Jazzercise, my ratio of saying yes to opportunities that presented themselves versus no was probably 25:1. When in doubt, I'd check my gut and, mostly, charge ahead with great passion and enthusiasm. When you're just getting started, it makes sense to do whatever you can to get the word out, grow the business, ride the initial wave of success as fast and as far as you can.

But there is a point when that ratio of yes to no needs to consciously change. It may come when your success begins to attract the attention of others whose ideas, interests, or intentions don't necessarily parallel yours. Proceed with caution when anyone suggests they know your business better than you do. And, hopefully, you'll avoid mistakes like the ones I made.

By 1985, Jazzercise was well past the start-up stage. We had franchisees in all 50 states and 17 foreign countries, and a grand new corporate headquarters that included dance studios, a JMTV recording studio, plus a warehouse for our burgeoning Jazzertogs division. We also had several high-priced consultants eager to help us "explore new revenue sources."

> *"The future of Jazzercise is in custom-built studio centers that include a JazzerGym for toddlers."*
>
> ⸺Fancy, big-bucks consultant number one

One guy got my attention when he showed up with a child development expert armed with toddler-sized balls, blocks, and climbing things. While he explained how adding gym play to the Jazzercise mix would be both a help to our customers with young children and a boon to our bottom line, I watched my own two-and-a-half-year-old Brendan climb and jump and tumble with the gym toys. The huge smile on his face really got me and, despite some inner misgivings, I gave the go-ahead to design and build out two prototype centers in Irvine, California, and Reston, Virginia. I even authorized a photo shoot for posters and marketing materials that included Brendan, of course. Our thinking was if these two prototypes proved successful, we'd consider a nationwide rollout.

After an extended period of lease negotiations, local planning department approvals, and construction, I was invited to visit the new JazzerGym/Studio in Irvine and was horrified. By misplacing the emphasis on the needs of the kids, the studio space was too small and chopped up, the sight lines for adult students to follow their Jazzercise instructor impossible. A quick trip to Reston revealed the same immutable mistakes. In focusing on Brendan's playful response, instead of my own gut feelings, I'd made a big and very expensive mistake. I had no choice but to pull the plug on both centers, take the hit, and move on. Lesson learned, I thought. While indoor gyms for kids are a valid business for some, they didn't quite match up with ours. Remember, nobody knows your business better than you do. You must stay true to who you are.

> *"If you're looking for easy additional revenue, why don't you do an infomercial?"*
>
> ⸱⸱⸱Fancy, big-bucks consultant number two

In the 1990s, Jack and JMTV had produced a library of award-winning Jazzercise videotapes for at-home use, including our bestselling *Simply Jazzercise*, *Power Workout*, and *Body Sculpting*. Our videotape sales were mostly to existing customers through our Jazzertogs catalogs shipped regularly to all Jazzercise instructors for in-studio, after-class distribution. As always, our marketing team was on the hunt for ways to expand our reach and sales.

Enter another round of MBAs. (Nothing against MBAs

but, in my previous painful experience, I'd learned nobody knows your business better than you do, right?) Once again, after much study, review, and discussion, our expensive hired guns concluded they'd discovered the perfect way to dramatically increase product sales.

The big idea on the table was to produce and run an infomercial for Jazzercise at-home videos. The product already existed, so no cost there. We needed only to hire the experts to write and produce the infomercial to exacting infomercial standards (which were supposedly beyond the capabilities of our own JMTV division), fund an extensive run on the infomercial channel, and watch the orders and additional revenue roll in.

Almost everyone on my management and marketing team said, "That sounds like a pretty cool idea!"

I thought, "Hmm, I don't know . . ." Inside, my gut was churning. Jazzercise had always been *people*-based, not *product*-based. We did have products, but our main source of income sprang from the in-class connection with our customers, with other people. While we had always been about moving people, this infomercial was solely about moving product, and it just didn't feel right to me. I should have said no, but I didn't.

Another long painful story short, the infomercial's production costs ate up most of the allotted half-a-million-dollar budget, which was supposed to cover airtime as well. The few times it did run, it flopped. And to add insult to injury, the producer made my then–VP of Marketing a job offer she couldn't refuse. We lost both the money and our talented head of marketing!

Stay present in your business. Watch for the cues, signs, and signals that indicate a correction is required. Resist the urge or pressure from others to leap before you're ready. Take the time to learn how to be proactive instead of simply reactive. And remember, even the best dancers stumble; their only choice is to recover, find the beat again, and move on.

CHAPTER 4

CLEF NOTES

♪ Watch for the ways your business alerts you through cues, signs, and signals to situations requiring thoughtful, sometimes immediate attention. Resolve to make sure your response is proactive instead of simply reactive.

♪ As an entrepreneur, the passion and protectiveness you have for your business can feel a lot like the love you have for your family. Although it may be difficult to allow others to take care of something you hold so dear, your success may make it impossible not to let go of sole control. Recast this in your mind as a good thing.

♪ Listen to your gut, that inner voice that encompasses all your passion, experience, strength, talents, skills, mishaps, and learned lessons. When something doesn't sit right with you, listen to your hesitation. Take the time to think it through. Proceed only when your inner voice agrees. It will never steer you wrong.

♪ Despite its often-daunting up-front expense, investing in technology that fuels growth, improves performance, simplifies production or processes, and/or streamlines communication between your company teams, customers, or target audiences can prove well worth the cost in the long run.

♪ One success often leads to another. By that I mean that a success in one area may create the opportunity to expand in another area that wasn't obvious before. Keep your eyes open to the possibilities.

♪ The more successful you become, the more people will show up to pair up, partner, or propose their ideas on how they can make you better. Not to steer you away from high-priced and/or expert consultants, but always remember that nobody knows your business as well as you do.

Growing Organically, Going Viral . . . and Global

When the opportunity to grow presents itself, my philosophy is if my gut says go, let's go. By the time others complete their analysis of the situation, the opportunity may be gone.

TO PLAN, OR NOT TO PLAN?

There's an ongoing argument in entrepreneurial circles. On one side, the planners believe the first requirement of any entrepreneurial venture is a detailed three- to five-year business plan. On the other side are what I'd call the "seat-of-your-pantsers," who favor a "let's just do it and see where it goes" approach.

> *"Start with a simple idea that can help a lot of people . . . and let it grow naturally."*
> —Nicholas Tart, business writer

For decades, I've readily admitted that when I started Jazzercise, the idea of a business plan never occurred to me. What mattered was my passion and purpose and aligning myself with others who felt the same way. A few years back, business writer Nicholas Tart published a list of ten billion-dollar companies that didn't start with a business plan either. The list includes Google, Yahoo, Apple, Facebook, General Electric, Disney, Pepsi, Nike, Cisco, and Walmart.

So, we're in good company.

Which is not to say business plans aren't important—we have one now—but rather, to prove they're not *always* necessary. Instead, as Nicholas Tart suggests, what's most important is to "start with a simple idea that can help a lot of people" and "let it grow naturally."

WHEN AND WHERE YOU START YOUR BUSINESS MATTERS

Hindsight is 20/20, right? Looking back, I can see clearly the extraordinary confluence of four key factors that helped boost the dramatic takeoff of Jazzercise in 1977. My hope, in briefly recounting them, is to provide you with food for thought on the timing and location for beginning your venture.

> "Boy, were we in the right place at the right time!"
>
> ⸺First full-time employee and future chief operating officer Margaret Stanton

For starters, the 1977 US economy was in full recovery mode after the deep recession of 1973–75. Production, employment, and consumer spending were all up, and the mood of the country—having put Watergate, President Nixon, and Vietnam firmly behind us—was generally upbeat. Of course, I'm not saying you should wait until everything's rosy to start your business; but having survived five recessions since then, I'd say it's always better to have a steady economic wind filling your sails (and sales) than not. This is especially true when you're introducing something nobody's ever heard of before, as we were back then.

Second, consider the prevailing spirit, mood, or "zeitgeist" of your core audience. For us, by 1977 the women's movement had gained widespread traction with the idea that a woman was entitled to take a bit of time off from her regular duties—worrying about the house, the car, the kids, the laundry, the boss or being a boss—to "do something for yourself." For many women, 55 minutes of Jazzercise twice a week was that gateway "something." They came, they had fun, they looked great, they felt great afterward, they invited their friends to join them, and they made new friends as well. In addition to greater fitness, most of our customers reported greater self-confidence—a progression that inspired many to seek training as a certified Jazzercise instructor and independent businesswoman. Does your business concept dovetail with the prevailing spirit among your core customers? Are there ways to improve your "fit"? For example, to boost our customers' ability to attend class, we provided child care, when needed, during class times. We still do, because it works for them and for us.

Thirdly, is the place where you're starting your business easily accessed by early adopters and influencers, as well as your larger ideal audience? Although I enjoyed initial success at the prestigious Giordano Studios in Chicago, our move to health- and body-conscious Southern California proved extremely fortuitous. Interest in an exciting, new fitness option was high, and it was augmented by an active lifestyle in fine year-round weather. Further, in addition to attracting local permanent residents, our classes were very popular with military families, both women in the military and wives of husbands temporarily assigned to one of the many military bases in the area. As this particularly mobile audience moved on, they would fuel demand for Jazzercise in other states and countries. Of course, the Internet can radically compress the distance between companies and their customers. Even on the worldwide web, however, you must consider that your launch and location lands in the best, most fertile digital neighborhoods.

Finally, as I mentioned in the previous chapter, accessing and adapting the latest technology was and remains a huge boon for us. Back then, it was VHS taping, duping, and distribution. Today, it's live-streamed training, up-to-the-minute website updates, constant social media contact with customers, and immediate proprietary web channel communication with our franchisees. I understand starting on a shoestring, but I'd urge you to carefully weigh the cost-benefit of the best available technology, and to consider scrimping elsewhere.

DRAMATIC GAINS AND GROWING PAINS

Imagine this: after eight years as the Jazzercise one-woman band, I was suddenly thrust into the role of leader and chief decision-maker for 10 eager, energetic, newly minted in-structors with many more women calling or joining us in our 500-square-foot office. Margaret Stanton, our one full-time employee, handled the phone and the office, expertly fielding the near-constant requests for additional classes, additional instructors, in additional areas outside San Diego County.

Sounds like a great problem to have, right? I thought so, too. But scaling the business from one instructor (me), to 11, to 30 by the end of one year was not without some classic start-up challenges.

In truth, I was a seat-of-my-pantser who had somehow climbed aboard a rocket and was steering "with my gut." My good fortune was the ability (learned from my mother) to problem solve on the fly, combined with the steadying pres-ence of Margaret, who had both a degree and experience in business administration, and topped off with the inherent (though previously untested) talents of our First Ten, who were as committed to the cause as I was.

Growing Pain #1:
Replacing seat-of-the-pants selection with a standardized training process

I handpicked the first ten instructors based on my own gut-level metric, which included the following:

- Physical ability to dance

- The skill of quickly mastering choreography

- Emotional energy

- Enthusiasm

- Patience

- Compassion to lead a group of mostly nondancers through a fun and fitness-producing 55-minute class

- The intellectual acuity and ambition to develop, market, and manage one's own class schedule and independent business

Clearly, given my mushrooming demands, we needed a more formal selection and training process. My solution was an "all-hands-on-deck" brainstorming session with the First Ten plus Margaret to create a workable teacher training expansion plan. The result (which is similar to what we use today) was a series of two to three highly structured workshops run by existing instructors to identify, test, train, and certify potential candidates. Initially, all workshops occurred in Carlsbad. As we grew, we discovered the process was portable, which enabled training teams to travel and expanded our national and international markets to conduct new instructor certification workshops on-site.

It can be challenging to impose structure on a previously seat-of-the-pants process, especially if you're the hands-on founder. But your almost immediate rewards will be higher efficiency, better predictability, and, most important, the scalability that yields greater and faster growth.

In musical terms, the tempo of that time sped quickly from *moderato* (moderate speed) to *vivacissimo* (very fast and lively). By the end of that year, the First Ten had become the Original Thirty, and just two years after that, we'd reached 100. In three years, we were at 640 and by the five-year mark, we had 1,650 certified Jazzercise instructors. These numbers were well beyond what I might have projected in a business plan, if we'd had one.

Growing Pain #2:
Providing a calm, clear-sighted center while navigating the storm

When you're an entrepreneur whose business has finally made it past the product design/market fit phase, and you're moving quickly into scaling for a much larger audience, there's a tremendous sense of exhilaration. You're in the thrall of creating something completely new, not quite knowing where you're going nor exactly what you're doing, and yet you are still discovering and improving at every turn.

Harvard Business School pinpoints the most frequent

sticking point for a small but growing business as the owner's managerial ability and "willingness to delegate responsibility" to others. I didn't have an MBA, from Harvard or anywhere else, but I did have the common sense to embrace the big directional decisions while delegating the management of other key tasks to competent people.

I felt my role was to identify and prioritize *what* needed to be done, encourage those team members *who* were most capable and motivated to take on the task, then step aside and empower them to figure out *how* to do it. For example, I had been teaching several local kids' classes called Junior Jazzercise. The kids loved it, the parents loved it, and I felt strongly the program could be grown and scaled systemwide. First Ten instructor Kathleen Acri had a natural and inspired affinity for teaching kids and, at my urging, took on Junior Jazzercise with gusto. She perfected the structure, a combo of classes and performances; presented it at our conventions; and promoted it into a very popular add-on for franchisees across the country and around the world. Similarly, her dynamic sister Claudia took on the college audience and later expanded the key LA/Pasadena market. Karen Halley, another First Ten, took on and captured the lucrative Orange County market. In each of these instances, I set the priorities and picked the right people, and these three extraordinary women proved more than capable of turning opportunities into very successful realities for us.

Delegating many of the day-to-day details to others freed me to concentrate on the bigger picture, to monitor our overall direction, create and tend to our company culture, and make sure that in the middle of very rapid growth we were staying true to our core values. (There's more about this in Chapter 8, "Create a Purposeful Culture.")

Growing Pain #3:
Hiring outside talent versus promoting from within

Rapid growth and change can be challenging. Many business experts recommend hiring the talent you need from the outside. Conversely, I'm a longtime proponent of rechanneling the talent and passion that already exists within our ranks. It's a choice you'll have to make when you're scaling up.

As a wide variety of challenges surfaced during our critical first few years, one by one, members of our intrepid First Ten stepped out of their teaching comfort zones to help. I offer these anecdotes as proof that often the solutions to some of your team's more insistent problems are as close as an enterprising team member.

Problem/Solution: Hands-on management of our rapidly mushrooming team

When, for example, we hit 38 certified instructors, with dozens more in the pipeline, popular First Ten instructor Nikki Miller applied to become our first director of instructors. "Basically, my job was keeping track of everyone," Nikki explains, "to get to know all the teachers personally, help with their particular needs, and let them know what worked for others." Recalling her motivation at the time, Nikki says, "I saw the organization growing and I wanted to grow with it." She did. And when a family move forced Nikki to leave us, her replacement, fellow instructor Jan Kinney, directed our growth from 100 to more than 5,000 instructors over the next 25 years.

Problem/Solution: Bestselling book research and coordination

When one of my students, Dona Z. Meilach, approached me to explain that she was a professional writer of popular how-to books—"I think your message would be a great how-to book!"—First Ten's detail-oriented Katrina Wolf stepped in to coordinate the flow of information, explanation of terms, directions, and photographs that made the book a reality. Without Katrina's help and her patient attention to detail, our first international bestseller with versions in English, French, Spanish, Dutch, and German might never have happened.

Problem/Solution: Coordinating publicity and public relations

After the book *JAZZERCISE: A Fun Way to Fitness* came out in May 1978, our already busy little office was overwhelmed by a blizzard of phone calls from newspapers, magazines, and others requesting information about Jazzercise, interviews, and appearances. First Ten's dynamic Mary Nuckles MacGyver volunteered to help and proved to be a PR wizard. That May, at Jack's suggestion, I drove up to NBC's studio in Los Angeles to present a copy of the book to the producer of Dinah Shore's popular TV show. Her response was positive but vague. "Love to have you," she said, "but no dates are currently available. We'll give you a few days' notice when we have an opening." Over the next 10 months, Mary called, checked in, and sent letters, copies of the book, press updates—whatever she could think of—to remind the producer of her offer. Finally, in March 1979, we received a date. Unfortunately, it conflicted with an unbreakable commitment I had in Florida. To her credit, Mary persisted and in May 1979, one year after my initial visit to the studio, I was invited back for my first appearance on national television.

When we arrived on set, I was directed to the makeup room while the show's producer invited Mary into her office. "Do you want to know why your boss is on 'Dinah!' today?" she asked. "Sure," Mary said. "Because you are the most tenacious PR person I've ever seen," the producer said. Turning to her bookcase, she removed seven of the eight copies of our book from her shelf and handed the stack to Mary. "Here," she said, "please use these to pester someone else."

Soon, the airing of my visit to 'Dinah!' led to appearances on the widely syndicated John Davidson and Phil Donahue shows, as well as dozens of "Judi's Jazzercise" segments on Westinghouse's "PM/Evening Magazine." When you are in need of a public relations wizard for your scaling business, I hope you'll remember how Mary Nuckles MacGyver's relentless tenacity vaulted Jazzercise onto the nationwide stage.

Problem/Solution: Acquiring dance music records, tapes, and CDs

One big issue for our busy instructors was getting their hands on the musical records (45s and LPs) that my choreography required them to play in class. Often, a group would carpool to Tower Records in San Diego or Los Angeles and find there weren't enough copies for everyone. After several frustrating trips, resourceful First Ten instructor Judy Ritter stepped forward to offer her fellow teammates, "Look, what if I take the list of Judi's new songs, call up Tower Records, or wherever, and group order what we all need? I'll charge each of you the cost of the records plus five dollars for me. Deal?"

Over time, while Margaret negotiated music rights for our routines, Judy Ritter's efforts evolved from securing records to cassette tapes to CDs for all Jazzercise instructors everywhere. When digital downloads replaced CDs, Judy retired from her musical distribution business to go into local politics. Today, she is the third-term mayor of Vista, California. "Jazzercise gave me skills—public speaking, business management, contract negotiation—that I continue to use every day."

Problem/Solution: Communicating companywide news, ideas, and updates

During times of rapid growth, it is critical to have an effective channel to communicate companywide news, updates, shared successes, and/or educational failures efficiently and transparently with everyone. When Jack suggested but had no time to write or produce a company newsletter, wise and witty Mary "Mare" James, another First Ten instructor, took on the task of collecting, documenting, writing, proofreading, and coordinating "all the news that's fit!" with the graphic artist and printer. Today, companies communicate digitally, as we do, but the essence is the same. I sincerely hope you find someone who will make your intracompany news and views as entertaining, educational, and relatable as Mare James did ours. While technology is terrific for facilitating a variety of messaging to different markets—we use e-newsletters and a web portal to communicate weekly with our instructors, web pages and social media to connect regularly with our customers, and seasonal email blasts to inform our apparel fans of new collections—there's no replacing the human heart and voice that creates and keeps the communication real and meaningful.

Growing Pain #4:
Scaling *esprit de corps,* maintaining the sense of fellowship

In the earliest days of a company, there's an intimacy, a definite *esprit de corps* among the team members who are first to sign on in support of your mission. Challenges are openly discussed and debated; victories small and large wildly celebrated; personal relationships effortlessly established and maintained. Often, as you grow and expand across multiple work sites, states, or regions, there's a real loss of the easy exchanges between different departments, and a formality is imposed by systems meant to track accountability and commitment. How do you gain and enjoy the benefits of scaling without losing the sense of fellowship that got you there?

My answer, from the beginning till now in our fiftieth year, is a quarterly corporate meeting with everyone included. Whether that means in person, via satellite, or digital sign-in, every Jazzercise team member—from receptionists to the complete executive team—attends this meeting. Generally, we prepare ahead of time by emailing a request to all departments for pertinent discussion topics, news, updates, or challenges to be shared. At the meeting, we welcome newbies, acknowledge significant milestones, restate strategic priorities, update existing initiatives, celebrate accomplishments, and discuss future plans. Our aim is always to reaffirm our communal purpose, strengthen individual and cross-departmental connections, and sustain complete transparency. It is not as difficult as it sounds if you, as head of the company, make it a priority.

Further, in my experience, there's no bigger or better shot in the communal arm than a live companywide celebration of significant milestones. By late 1982, five years after my decision to certify other instructors, we had reached some mightily impressive benchmarks: we'd grown dramatically from the First Ten in Southern California to 1,650 certified instructors and more than 300,000 customers in 46 states and 12 foreign countries. We'd not only navigated the IRS- and accounting-imposed transition from independent contractors to franchisees without a single lost relationship; we'd also become the second-fastest growing franchisor in the United States, just behind Domino's Pizza. In addition, our book *JAZZERCISE: A Fun Way to Fitness* had become an international bestseller, and our *Jazzercise* record album, the first-ever dance exercise album, was certified gold by MCA. (It later went platinum.) *And* I was happily pregnant with our long-desired second child.

We were in the mood to celebrate and invited every instructor to join us for the first Jazzercise International Instructors' Convention in Carlsbad, California. Fully three-quarters of them came. It was a three-day weekend, packed with expert workshops, food, entertainment, and fun. On

Sunday, we invited 3,000 local customers, all of us filling the football field of a local college, and we danced.

In a big surprise for the crowd, the original Spinners joined me on stage singing live while we danced our popular routines for "Working My Way Back," "Cupid," "Rubber Band Man," and others. In the grand finale, championship bodybuilder Charles Bradshaw flexed his muscles while I led the group through "Eye of the Tiger" and—another huge surprise—a live 200-pound tiger named Asia prowled across the stage behind me. At the end, everyone applauded as thousands of multicolored balloons were released, and a small plane appeared overhead to skywrite *JAZZERCISE*. That event—a true meeting of minds and gathering of hearts—generated such synergy and *esprit de corps* that we've convened similar live milestone celebrations in every decade since.

Although live tigers and skywriting airplanes may not be appropriate for your business, I urge you to celebrate your communal successes with all the people who made them happen. The layers of meaningful outcomes will surprise and delight you and may well make achieving your next milestone possible.

GOING VIRAL . . . AND GLOBAL

I'm often asked to explain the phenomenal growth of Jazzercise in our first decade. The best way to describe it is "a magnetic moment," which in scientific terms occurs when a magnet both produces its own internal magnetic field and

> *"Jazzercise went viral long before anyone knew what 'going viral' was."*
>
> ⁓Jazzercise president
> Shanna Missett Nelson

draws or is drawn to other external magnetic fields. Our program's passion and purpose drew exceptional women of talent, ability, and ambition. My decision was to give them the opportunity, training, and, perhaps most important, permission to apply their own passion and purpose to attract others elsewhere. For the most part, our people succeeded beyond their and our wildest dreams. "Don't be afraid, don't overthink," I told them. "Just listen to your gut, follow your heart, and you'll find a way to get it done." To their everlasting credit, then and now, they did and do.

These days, everyone wants his or her business to "go viral." For Jazzercise, our explosive growth, in every state and 25 foreign countries, was never the result of one core business strategy or one wildly successful marketing plan. On the contrary, we are a consortium of separate businesses run by individual owners given great flexibility and freedom to succeed in their own market in their own way.

Of course, our franchisees share similar branding and receive the same core product—continually updated dance routines choreographed to contemporary music—plus extensive training and corporate support. Beyond that, they've been exceptionally creative and tenacious in building their independent success. The following case studies are meant to provide you with insights into how three different Jazzercise entrepreneurs succeeded using three widely different strategies and plans.

Case Study #1:
Connecting with Key Celebrity Influencers in Ohio

Jeri Sipe was a petite, sandy-haired cheerleader who'd married the quarterback—San Diego State's Brian Sipe, the nation's leading collegiate passer in his senior year. After Brian was drafted by the Cleveland Browns, he and Jeri moved part-time to Ohio, returning off-season to their home in North San Diego County. In late summer 1978, Jeri, one of our dynamic Original Thirty instructors, approached me with a question. "I'm heading to Cleveland soon. Should we try Jazzercise there?" she asked. "Why not?" I replied, eager to see how Jazzercise would fare outside Southern California.

The small bedroom community of Medina, Ohio, population 15,307, was home to a number of Brian's Cleveland Browns teammates and other professional athletes. After securing space and posting flyers at the county community center, Jeri had 13 women show up for her first class in September. By December, she had 300 students (several pro athletes' wives among them) in 11 classes. She'd also trained three additional local teachers, the talented Betty Sanford, Marta Sherk, and Fran Auker. Fran had a twin sister in West Virginia who wanted to teach, too. Soon, Jeri, Betty, Marta, and Fran had trained 38 instructors from several Cleveland suburbs (Hudson, Brunswick, Wadsworth, Lodi), Cleveland proper, Toledo, and Akron, plus Fran's sister Jean from

West Virginia, and a few others who drove down from Michigan.

Meanwhile, quarterback Brian and his Browns team-mates were providing Cleveland fans with so many heart-stopping moments on the football field, they'd earned the nickname the "Kardiac Kids." When, in 1980, Brian's record-setting performance earned him the NFL MVP award, he and Jeri resolved to use their influence "to do some good." A series of 16 high-profile charity events around the state, featuring appearances by Brian, his fel-low Browns players, and their Jazzercising wives, not only raised $62,000 for the Mental Health Association of Ohio but also significantly elevated interest in Jazzercise Ohio. In 1984 and '85, Brian and his teammates, and Jeri and their wives, came together again, this time for Jazzercise with the Stars, back-to-back celebrity fund-raisers in honor of young Browns fan Robyn Schafer and United Cerebral Palsy (UCP) of Greater Cleveland. The combined $90,000 for UCP they raised benefited everyone involved, includ-ing Jazzercise Ohio. Other franchisees in other states took note. Many followed Jeri's successful lead and continue to do so to this day. (See details in Chapter 11, "The Joy of Giving Back.")

Case Study #2:
Securing Governmental Support and Statewide Press Coverage in New Mexico

In 1978, DeeDee Kovacevich was the girls' physical education teacher at Oceanside's El Camino High School when she approached Margaret and me about incorporating Jazzercise into the school's curriculum. The following spring of 1979, after making Jazzercise the most popular class on campus, DeeDee returned to say, "My husband and I have decided to move to Santa Fe, New Mexico. Of course, I'd like to take Jazzercise with me. And here's something else: My colleague at ECHS used to play football with Jerry Apodaca, who's not only the governor of New Mexico but also on the President's Council on Physical Fitness. My one-year goal is to use that connection to get Judi and Jazzercise recognized by the President's Council."

Six weeks later, after several unsuccessful attempts, DeeDee wrangled both an introduction and an appointment to meet with Apodaca at the state capitol. By that time, he was concluding his second term as governor and was about to begin a new role as chairman of the President's Council on Physical Fitness and Sports. "When he heard what Jazzercise was and saw the articles which had been written about us, he invited us to present the program in Washington, DC, at the next council meeting," DeeDee explains. "I told Judi I wanted to get her to Washington within a year. It only took a month and a half!"

That September 1979, a group of Jazzercise veterans—Californians Kathleen Acri, Nikki Miller, and Cindy Luxton, Virginia instructor Chelle Tierney, my 11-year-old daughter Shanna, and I—performed and received a terrific response from the council, as well as *The Washington Post* and NBC News. "The Jazzercise part really livened things up," Chairman Apodaca said.

Starting with two classes and 40 students at Los Alamos, DeeDee soon expanded with several classes in Santa Fe. One of her students was Anne Hillerman, daughter of the popular New Mexican mystery novelist Tony Hillerman and a writer herself for the *Santa Fe New Mexican*, the oldest newspaper in the West. Anne wrote a story about DeeDee and Jazzercise that included a glowing review, large photos, and DeeDee's home phone number. About the same time, DeeDee's newly trained instructor Janece Blake contacted the *Albuquerque Journal*. One week later, a full-page story ran in the state's largest paper and again included DeeDee's number.

"My phone was ringing off the hook from cities I'd never heard of—Pojoaque, Corrales, Espanola, White Rock," she said. "I had no template but, piece by piece, we figured it out."

Within months, the mayor of Albuquerque declared February 10, 1980, "Jazzercise Day." When I flew in to join the celebration, 15 New Mexico instructors greeted me with a performance of "We Are Fam-i-ly" in the corridors of the airport. In Los Alamos, I met 400 students, in Santa Fe, 800 students, followed by a supersized celebration at the Albuquerque Convention Center with 1,650 New Mexican customers.

Sandwiched between these events were radio, television, and newspaper interviews, a luncheon with local recreation and community education directors, and an award ceremony from the New Mexico Governor's Council on Physical Fitness and Sports.

"And don't forget our gorgeous Jazzercise hot-air balloon," DeeDee says, "a real highlight at Albuquerque's annual Balloon Festival."

DeeDee pieced things together so well that, by 1985, she was our area director for the far west, including Nevada, California, Oregon, Washington State, Alaska, and Hawaii.

Case Study #3:
Grassroots/Guerrilla Marketing
in Rural Wisconsin

Peggy Leinenkugel's husband, Jake, was a US Marine sergeant temporarily assigned to Oceanside's Camp Pendleton. At her very first Jazzercise class, a television news crew showed up to film several new teachers and filmed Peggy as well. "The thought hit me," Peggy said, "that 'maybe I could teach this.' But, unfortunately, the cost of the training workshop was $75, which we didn't have." That weekend, she emptied the large jar where she and Jake saved spare change and the contents added up, almost exactly, to $75. "I considered it a sign," Peggy said.

Not long after she was certified in January 1979, Jake was selected for Officer Candidate School on the East Coast. Together they decided that, while Jake attended OCS, Peggy and their two kids would return home to Chippewa Falls, Wisconsin, population 12,270. "When I told Jake I planned to teach Jazzercise there, he laughed. 'In Chippewa? That's never going to work,' he said."

Hugely motivated by Jake's challenge, Peggy visited Bill Feherty, head of the local Parks and Rec Department. "I've studied your class schedule and it appears everything you're offering is for men. Why not add something for women?" she asked. When Feherty agreed, Peggy made up 200 flyers announcing her new class.

"The challenge was to reach the women. How? You may laugh but my thought was, 'Where do women feel most uncomfortable with their bodies?' And my conclusion was . . . on the toilet and in store dressing rooms."

Peggy visited all the local stores where women shopped and secured permission to hang her flyers in their dressing rooms. Then she drove to the popular Van's Supper Club and approached owner Van Verbrecken about posting flyers in the restaurant's ladies' room stalls. "Mr. Verbrecken was wonderful and really appreciated that this might be something women would want," Peggy recalls. "He even suggested the best places to put my flyers for maximum visibility."

As the date of the first class approached, Peggy worried whether Jake was right, what if nobody came? That night, 80 women showed up. Within a few months, she had 300 students in Chippewa Falls, with another 400 in nearby Eau Claire, and was receiving calls from Milwaukee, Green Bay, Madison, Stevens Point, and Minneapolis. Within a few years, Peggy became our area director for nine central states—Wisconsin, Illinois, Iowa, Minnesota, North and South Dakota, Kansas, Nebraska, Michigan—plus western Canada.

And what was Jake's response to Peggy's success? "I was shocked!" he said. "In northwestern Wisconsin, women kept coming. I learned to never doubt my wife's abilities again."

Case Studies #4–8,500: Always Encourage—and Leave Room for—Others' Creativity, Innovation, and Success

Successful women like Jeri Sipe in Ohio, DeeDee Kovacevich in New Mexico, and Peggy Leinenkugel in Wisconsin inspired many other Jazzercise entrepreneurs. I could easily add the case studies of Barbara Morris, Cathy McKenzie, and Priscilla Dunkel in Texas, Barbara Strausbaugh, Barrie Rakow, and Cheryl Wiggins in Florida, and on and on in the successful expansion of Jazzercise in each of the 50 states.

I could also recount the particular challenges and creative solutions when many of our military-affiliated instructors received transfers, and took Jazzercise with them, to their new postings in Okinawa, Japan; Ankara, Turkey; Rome; Geneva; Sydney; Guam; Fiji; and Curitiba, Brazil. Dance is a universal language, so my choreography translated easily. But each base and each expansion into the surrounding culture was specifically different and required lots of creative problem solving and hard, hard work in-country. These women amazed

> *"A movement is only composed of people moving. To feel its warmth and motion around us is the end as well as the means."*
>
> ⸺Gloria Steinem, author of *Outrageous Acts and Everyday Rebellions*

us, then and now, with their tenacious innovations and adaptations.

As CEO of a rapidly growing enterprise, global or otherwise, one of your major decisions may well revolve around the question of trust. How much control do you retain at the corporate level versus how much leeway do you provide those "in the field" and "on the ground"? In five decades of global management, I have always erred on the side of trust. Choose your people wisely, make sure their passion and purpose align with yours, train them well, then encourage, empower, and trust them to chart your shared success. It has, with a few, exceedingly rare exceptions, always worked for Jazzercise, and for me.

CLEF NOTES

♪ If you're a planner, go ahead and make your three-to five-year business plan. I wish you great success. If you're a "seat-of-your-pantser," like me, there's plenty of validity in "let's just do it and see where it goes." Considering that Walt Disney, Steve Jobs, and Mark Zuckerberg, among many others, had no plan when they began their billion-dollar ventures, you'll be in good company.

♪ As eager as you are to get started, the timing and location of your start-up, the prevailing mood or "zeitgeist" of your core audience, plus access to helpful technology are all factors that can impact your growth and success. It's more advantageous to be in sync with these factors than not.

♪ The first objective of any entrepreneur must be confirming the fit between your product and your market. I'm not saying you need to spend the eight years I spent perfecting the Jazzercise class format, but I know that one of the big reasons we were able to scale the concept so quickly and effectively is the time I'd spent working out all the kinks and doing my due diligence to confirm our market's sustainable demand beforehand.

♪ Scaling will take you and everyone else in your organization out of their comfort zone. If you're a "seat-of-your-pants" CEO, at some point you'll have to accept the need and responsibility for standardized processes, longer-term thinking and planning, and other organizing changes that are a part of the scaling process.

♪ As a start-up CEO of a scaling company, you will need to be the clear-eyed calm inside the storm. This will involve delegating much of the day-to-day decision-making to trusted others so you are free to confront head-on the larger issues that will impact the long term.

♪ Once you are in full scaling or, if you're fortunate, viral growth mode, you may mourn the earlier, easier days of start-up. Change is stressful and, if you're not careful, the structured accountability systems you need can deflate the *esprit de corps* everyone loved. Find ways to foster, maintain, and celebrate the human connections between work sites, departments, divisions, and corporate and field teammates. I'm a big fan of transparency and inclusion of people at meetings and events.

♪ Once you've carefully selected and trained the best people you can find to support your mission, encourage, empower, and, most important, trust their creativity, ambition, and expertise to deliver mutually beneficial success.

CHAPTER 6

Be a Rebel

March to your own beat. Being different can make all the difference.

C all me crazy—you wouldn't be the first—but I believe the shortest, fastest, most successful route to business innovation and change is not worrying about your competition, but simply, passionately attending to the needs of your customers.

At Jazzercise, we've had more competitors come and go than we could possibly count. Five decades later, we're still here—the largest franchised dance fitness company in the world, with the highest customer retention rates in the industry, and more than $2 billion in cumulative gross sales.

> *"The people who are crazy enough to think they can change the world, are the ones who do."*
>
> ⸺Steve Jobs

Why? Because we listen to our customers and continuously innovate to meet their needs. (Note that "needs" are not the same as "wants." As Steve Jobs famously said, "Nobody wanted an iPod until we convinced them they needed one.") And although innovation is hard, much harder than imitation, it is way more fun.

How did we do it? By disrupting the old conceptions, defying the existing hierarchy, and redefining fitness as a come-one, come-all, fun activity. Not that that's what we set out to do! But it is, in retrospect, where we wound up—by going with our guts and following our hearts.

Think about the difference between classical and jazz musicians. Classical musicians excel in their performance of existing notes on existing musical scores, many written centuries ago. They don't vary the notes—that's not allowed—but they do compete to see who plays the same score best. Jazz musicians do no such thing. They may start with an existing melodic line, but they rebel by improvising, adding notes and riffs of their own, and communing with other live jazz musicians to create something new and never heard before.

In my view, there are businesses that succeed in the way classical musicians do, by performing the status quo a bit better than others. And then there are businesses that, like jazz players, walk away from what already exists to create something new and that's never been seen before. Although both approaches are valid, when it comes to my business, I side with the more free-form jazz folks.

REBELS DISRUPT THE STATUS QUO

When I first started Jazzercise, fitness was in the nascent stages of what it is today. For men, most practices grew out of either military-style calisthenic training or Jack LaLanne–type muscle building plus supplements. Gyms were competitive male bastions, as women feared strength training might result in unattractive masculine musculature. The almost universal female goal at the time was to "slim down" or "reduce" (popular euphemisms for losing weight) through diet and minimal effort. The notion that exercise was a way for women to maintain good heart health, reduce stress, and "get fit" was neither widely known nor encouraged.

From the very first class in 1969, when my students turned away from the mirror, we disrupted the competitive tradition and pressures that existed in every dance studio, every gym, and every sports club in the country. We created instead a cooperative, communal space where everyone of every shape was welcome to discover the joy of jazz dance, to get fit, and to have fun. We were the first fitness organization to insist that challenging exercise can *and should be* fun.

> "*If you obey all the rules, you miss all the fun.*"
> —Actress Katharine Hepburn

And that was just the beginning. Many other fitness industry "firsts" followed. Some, deemed crazy at the time, are considered trailblazing and standard setting today. Rejecting the big gym scene, we pioneered the concept of "boutique fitness": smaller, more accessible, welcoming, neighborhood locations dedicated to group fitness. Renouncing competition, we built supportive customer communities full of encouragement, connection, and camaraderie. Forgoing expensive long-term membership contracts, we opted instead for affordable pay-as-you-go class fees and, when needed, we provided child care.

As an entrepreneurial rebel, you must consider these key questions: What is the status quo in your business concept's industry? Which sacred cows should be set aside in order to better meet your customers' needs? Which norms can you disrupt in order to create something entirely new?

REBELS SUBSUME THEIR EGOS IN PURSUIT OF A GREATER GOOD AND MORE LASTING IMPACT

Whoever you are, whatever your passion, whatever product, service, or company you hope to create and build, I urge you to see in your purpose something larger than yourself and to name your venture accordingly.

Who we are and what we do is Jazzercise, not "Judi Sheppard Missett's Jazz Dance for Fun and Fitness." While others in the fitness industry insisted on branding their efforts with their names, faces, bodies, and egos—creating expectations that their celebrity was central

> *"I am for those means which will give the greatest good to the greatest number."*
>
> ⸺Abraham Lincoln

to the delivery of their service or product, thereby limiting their long-term growth and impact to their own or the public's attention span—we became a movement that created opportunities for many individuals, be they customers or instructors.

As the first fitness program to train and certify instructors, and to franchise our methods, Jazzercise empowered our people to spread the benefits of the program wherever they chose to go. And our customers soon realized that, thanks to our pioneering use of video training and updates, they could enjoy a consistent, universal Jazzercise experience in many of the states and countries where they lived, visited, or vacationed. Along the way, we established the industry's first teaching and performance standards through our certification program, which continues to evolve today.

While my background was in the art of dance, an outstanding Jazzercise instructor in the early days was Peggy Marchbanks Buchanan, whose master's degree in physiology helped ground our movement in the science of safe exercise, perceived exertion, and good nutrition. Another co-rebel, Katie Gordon Parker, one of the most natural-born salespersons I've ever seen, generously contributed her profit-boosting ideas, expertise, and techniques to the cause as well.

Much as our self-named competitors relished the appearance of their faces and bodies on celebrity magazine covers, we relished our annual ranking in *Entrepreneur* magazine's Franchise 500 list of most successful franchises. It meant more women were empowered to start their own businesses, helping more people become fit every year. And it still does.

In the same way that a true rebel understands that rebellion is always a group activity seeking collective success, you must understand that your company is not about you. It is about your customers and the collective efforts of you and your co-rebels to meet their needs. Brand and lead your venture accordingly.

REBELS CREATE REACHABLE, SHAREABLE MOMENTS

In the beginning, most entrepreneurs scramble for ways to reach their customers. Advertising is expensive; sales promotion on a shoestring budget requires bold creativity.

In the early days of Nike, Phil Knight drove to track meets to sell his sleek, lightweight, Japanese-made running shoes out of the trunk of his car. Steve Wozniak showed off his first home-built computer, the Apple I, at Silicon Valley's Homebrew Computer Club, a connection that helped his partner Steve Jobs land their first contract for 100 preassembled machines with the Byte Shop, a local computer store.

> *"Fortune favors the bold."*
> ⸺Roman poet Virgil

In the earliest days of Jazzercise, I invited half a dozen of my students to join me at the local mall to demonstrate a few of our routines for holiday shoppers. As the music and our dancing attracted a crowd, Jack and our daughter, Shanna, walked around handing out flyers with info on available classes. We also performed at local fairs, at farmer's markets, and in the beach bandshell during peak summer holidays.

With a tweak of the adage "you can't make a silk purse out of a sow's ear," Jack and I jokingly called these events "Silk Purse Productions." Most of them paid off in a surge of class sign-ups.

As the company grew, our collective ideas for more and bigger demonstration events grew, too. In 1980, our first halftime show for the San Diego Chargers NFL team inspired other instructors around the nation to approach their town's NFL, NBA, and MLB teams with the offer of a free halftime or seventh-inning-stretch performance.

The success of those shows helped me convince renowned Broadway choreographer Ron Field that a contingent of Jazzercise dancers would be a great addition to the Opening Ceremonies of the 1984 Olympics in Los Angeles. What a thrill for nearly 300 of us, including instructors from all 50 states plus Germany, Japan, Sweden, and Italy, to be a part of that historic happening and to expose Jazzercise to a global TV audience of two and a half *billion* viewers. In the years since, we've been a part of the dazzling rededication of the Statue of Liberty in New York Harbor as well as the Orange Bowl in Miami, the Super Bowl in San Diego, and innumerable national and international parades, fairs, festivals, and sporting events.

Of course, today we—and you—have many more avenues to reach out and promote ourselves to our audience. As with our earliest efforts, when you're short on funds, you must go long and big on creativity to garner attention and comment. Social media platforms offer excellent opportunities to affordably attract and engage existing and potential customers. In your pursuit of social media exposure, my advice is to focus on the value over the volume of your content; and to aim for topics that will educate or entertain your audience.

REBELS DREAM BIG AND WORK THEIR BUTTS OFF TO MAKE THEIR DREAM A REALITY

Rebellion is not the easy path, not by a long shot. Big dreams require a tremendous amount of persistence and hard work. Pulling off the dream of a lifetime—performing at the Olympics Opening Ceremonies, on the most-watched stage on earth—was one of the hardest things we've ever done, yet it was also one of the most rewarding.

In my experience, even the biggest dreams can be broken down into small, doable steps. First, you must envision it. Whatever your dream, you must see it clearly and internalize it as distinctly as possible. If you don't see it, hear it, feel its potential and possibility, no one else will either.

Jazzercise at the Olympics? We weren't athletes, we weren't competitors, we weren't even professional dancers in the dance world's strict definition. How dare we even dream, much less suggest, such a thing to the Tony award–winning, Broadway-choreographing legend of a man in charge? Yet, getting to and through the gate-

> *"A dream doesn't become reality through magic; it takes sweat, determination, and hard work."*
>
> —Colin Powell, statesman and four-star general

keeper is often the next logical step to making the dream happen.

I expected resistance, and I got it. "Jazzercise?" the great Ron Field asked me after I'd managed to wangle an appointment. "So you're a professional dance troupe?"

"Not in the traditional sense," I admitted. "But we are dancing professionals grounded in Gus Giordano's jazz dance techniques."

"And you can field a group of at least 250 dancers representing every state in the Union yet dancing together as one?"

"Yes, sir," I said, swallowing hard.

"How?"

"Well, first I'll master and videotape your routine, then ship the tapes to them. They'll learn it on their own, then everyone will come to California for three weeks of group rehearsals . . ."

"And costume fittings," he added.

"Exactly." I took his mention of costumes as a good sign. "Then, we'll all show up, looking good, looking great in fact, and perform exactly as planned."

In hindsight, once I got a look at his choreography notes, I would regret the words "exactly as planned." And I would have to approach the great man once again to ask, "Would it be all right if I simplified a few of the steps?"

"Simplify? How?"

"Well, we're going to be running up and down stairs and could use a couple more counts and repetitions to get everyone into position."

"Okay," he agreed. "But it's still going to look good?"

"Great, actually," I promised, with fingers crossed.

Not one of the steps that followed was easy, but they were worth it.

We'd promised at least 250 dancers and delivered 300. After weeks of intense individual and group preparation, on the day of the event, we performed as well as any professional dancing troupe on the planet. In fact, many of the national and international press reviews of the ceremonies specifically mentioned "the wonderful Jazzercise ladies." We could not have been more proud.

"Being there with my fellow Jazzercisers, having my family see the dress rehearsal, and performing with my teenage daughters in Olympic Stadium was one of the highlights of my life," Bobbi Janikas, one of our First Ten instructors, said. Mine, too, Bobbi.

Big dreams can be daunting, but that doesn't make them not doable. What's your big dream? Can you see it clearly enough to break it into manageable steps? Can you convince others to join you in the hard work required to make it happen? Are you prepared to answer the doubters who would have you edit or abandon your dream simply because it's never been done before? If your answer is an enthusiastic yes, then godspeed. You are well on your way.

REBELS KEEP THE FAITH, IN THEMSELVES AND OTHERS

To strive for excellence, to do things a bit differently is to stand out. To stand out is to invite attention, not all of it pleasant or good. In fact, the more you stand out the more some people will feel empowered to criticize, belittle, or attempt to tear you down.

At Jazzercise, we call the 1980s our Decade of Firsts. We were the first in the fitness industry to establish and accomplish so many things considered standard operating procedure today. As the nation's second-fastest-growing franchise, we were seemingly everywhere, widely noticed, and surprised to find ourselves occasionally derided for our aggressive commitment to make working out not just effective but fun. Yes, fun! Some of our critics had a field day with that.

> *"To be yourself in a world that is constantly trying to make you something else is the greatest accomplishment."*
>
> ⁓Ralph Waldo Emerson

Nevertheless, we persisted. (I love that phrase.) I think of the '80s as our teenage years—the decade between Jazzercise's tenth and twentieth years. Many people associate us with their youth (or their mother's or grandmother's youth) and are surprised to hear that we not only survived the '80s but have continued to grow, expand, and prosper in every decade since.

That's okay. We have never lost faith in ourselves or our

process. We have never shirked our commitment to our franchisees or shortchanged our customers in the delivery of serious exercise and dance choreography to popular music, served up with an overriding sense of fun and group camaraderie.

What we have done is grow and mature, as everyone must. We've changed with the times to stay on the cutting edge of fitness—adding multiple formats to Dance Mixx, the heart of our program, including strength training, a high-intensity interval program, a kickboxing option, a core-building class, and a strength-focused workout with weights, balls, and resistance bands. Among other formats and specialty classes, we have a "LO" program with low impact and strength training, and a Junior Jazzercise program for kids.

As my daughter, Shanna, now president of the company, explains, "Most fitness trends tend to come and go pretty quickly. They're quite popular and make their mark, then something else comes along. Our staying power is in the environment and community that we create with Jazzercise. It's welcoming and nonintimidating. We make people feel good about who they are, what they look like, whatever age they are. Our biggest competitor has always been the couch, not other fitness programs."

Call me crazy or rebellious—you wouldn't be the first. Make fun of fun, if you must. But never doubt that listening to your customers can result in innovative and revolutionary outcomes, regardless of what the competition is doing. And don't forget that being unconventional—standing out—feels good! We have made a difference by thinking, acting, and being different from everyone else.

CHAPTER 6
CLEF NOTES

♪ Even if you weren't born a rebel, you can become one by taking the path not chosen by everyone else in your industry. Different, disruptive businesses are the product of different, disruptive thinking. Don't be afraid to be different. It's what will make you and your business stand out to your customers as something special, unique, and innovative.

♪ Put your customers first in everything you do. Focus on meeting their needs, solving their problems, making their lives easier or better, or serving their greater good. It's a strategy that's worked for us for decades and is working for Amazon, Costco, Trader Joe's, and many others. Put your customers first, and they *will* return the favor.

♪ When funds are limited, you must dream big and creatively to get your ideas, products, or services out there. There will be plenty of folks who will doubt you, who will suggest you edit your dream or give it up as unachievable. Move past them to find your fellow rebels, those like-minded comrades willing to work their butts off beside you to make your shared dream a reality.

♪ As your business succeeds, grows, and matures, change is inevitable. Even if you're now leading the industry you once disrupted, or have survived decades, keep the faith in the passion and purpose that got you there. Return to the source—your customers—and find new, life-enriching ways to serve them.

Hard Yeses, Flexible Nos, and the Magical Power of *Why Not?*

Begin every negotiation with the firm belief that, together, you can find a way to a mutually beneficial agreement. Listen carefully. As in jazz, an improvisational response can produce a harmonious result.

Knowing how to negotiate is a critical skill in business and in life. Fortunately, it's a skill you can learn. Both my mother and my father came from a long line of farmers (Swedish and English/German) who appreciated a fair trade and a good barter. Each of my parents was an excellent negotiator, and I've applied their early lessons in my life and at Jazzercise for years.

MY FIRST LESSONS IN NEGOTIATING

When the only dance instructor in tiny Red Oak, Iowa, stopped teaching there, my mother visited every major dance studio in the big cities of Council Bluffs, Iowa, and Omaha, Nebraska, aiming to lure a new instructor to teach classes in our small town an hour away. "We need an instructor," she told them. "What do you need to make it worth your while?" Her detailed proposal—to secure space, market classes, sign up students, manage class paperwork, and assist with recitals—was designed to create "a winning situation" for both the out-of-town teacher and local students. My mom was personable yet tenacious, positive, and undeterred by multiple rejections. Ultimately, she succeeded in finding the exact right fit for everyone.

> *"Always strive for a winning situation."*
>
> ‑‑My parents,
> June and Del Sheppard

My father worked for the Army Corps of Engineers as liaison between the corps and the people whose lives were about to be impacted by a planned project. When an air force base in Michigan, for example, asked the corps to add another runway, it was my dad's job to visit each of the residents in the row of houses occupying the land where the new runway was to be built. His mission was to explain the right of eminent domain, the resident's need to move, and the government's overly fair financially but emotionally disappointing offer for their property. Dad's young assistant Dani Gilmore accompanied him on these homeowner appointments and shared, "He never delivered a canned speech. In fact, he approached each person with great empathy, listened carefully to their individual concerns, offered meaningful suggestions and alternatives, and usually managed to walk away with both their trust and their agreement."

My parents understood the importance of finding a solution that meets the needs of both parties. When negotiating, your aim should never be to push, or pull, or "put one over" on the other person. Instead, for a lasting agreement, you must simply and pleasantly listen and persist until, together, you find what they called "a winning situation." Which leads me to what we at Jazzercise call "hard yeses, flexible nos, and the magical power of *why not?*"

GETTING THE HARD YES

From the beginning of Jazzercise until now, an instructor's first priority is to find a location for his or her classes and negotiate a stable rent or lease. Because our class sites can range from public facilities managed by the local parks and rec departments to YMCAs, civic clubrooms, church community centers, school gyms, and proprietary Jazzercise Centers, each negotiation is unique.

> *"You not only have to understand fully what you believe and what your interests are but, in order to be a really good negotiator, you have to try to figure out what the other person on the other side of the table has in mind."*
>
> ---Former secretary of state
> Madeleine Albright

Although many of our franchisees are business-women with experience and confidence in their negotiating skills, many are budding entrepreneurs. Our training is designed to equip them with the tools to realistically assess how much rent they can afford to pay *before* they meet with a potential landlord. It makes zero sense to sit down to negotiate anything—a lease, a major purchase, a service contract, whatever—without prior knowledge of your own financial goals and limitations. Unfortunately, over the years, we have had some instructors who prematurely committed themselves to an unrealistic, untenable lease, dooming themselves to financial failure from the get-go. Their experiences can serve as a cautionary tale to every Jazzercise franchisee and business owner.

In addition to our franchisee's financial limitations as a potential tenant, each landlord has needs and limitations to consider as well *before* negotiations begin. Dani Gilmore Gresham, our US director of sales and my father's former assistant, explains it this way: "Whether it is with an individual person or with another business, getting a hard yes is about letting that person or business know what's in it for them. Preanalyzing their situation, confirming their needs face to face, enables you to point out what benefits you're bringing or offering *them* to improve, simplify, or make their situation more comfortable."

It's a common mistake to think that the negotiation, getting the hard yes, is all about money. It can be, but frequently it's not. Let me give you two examples.

Negotiating 101a: Spinning like windmills

When New Jersey instructor Sandra Langley approached Reverend Walter R. Coats about the possibility of teaching two classes a week in the Fellowship Hall of Trenton's First Presbyterian Church, he was somewhat reluctant to permit dance classes in venerable Titus Hall, established in 1712. Sandra countered by explaining how Jazzercise could help improve both the physical and mental health of Reverend Coats's female parishioners *and* how steady rent of the hall—at times when it would be otherwise empty—could help offset ongoing church expenses. After taking time to reflect, Reverend Coats not only agreed but also preached a sermon called "Jazzercise and the Gospel"! Here are a few excerpts from his remarks:

> "And then came another beat, the sounds of Jazzercise wafting up to my study through the innards of Titus Hall. Now some of you don't know about Jazzercise. It

came out of California, and for that I was a bit suspect of it. And it's intended to keep people—well, mostly women—in shape.

"No doubt some of my predecessors—[buried] in the sacred ground outside—are spinning like windmills as they watch these women enter church in their body stockings, carrying little mats or blankets. Indeed, some of us inside the building—and alive—are spinning.

"I don't know if it is a symbol of the modern church that—with oil bills climbing and insurance soaring—Jazzercise helps to bail us out!"

When presenting something new to a traditional or conservative client, it makes sense to maintain focus on mutual benefits, as Sandra did, and help them process the risk-reward equation. Together, Sandra Langley, Reverend Coats, and female parishioners of First Presbyterian arrived at their own winning situation.

Negotiating 101b: A paradigm shift at parks and recs

The challenge of getting a hard yes is usually convincing the deciding party that sometimes another way of doing things can work better for them than what they already have in place. Anyone seeking to sell to or partner with a bureaucracy that is set in its existing ways may relate.

We've run into this type of situation time and time again

with many different community parks and recreation departments where we hope to use their facilities to teach our classes. So, we go into each situation with a plan.

First, we analyze their current system and the advantages and disadvantages of their existing practices. Typically, parks and recs hire fitness instructors at a set hourly rate for a limited six- to eight-week session. The advantage of this practice is inexpensive labor. The disadvantages are a lack of quality control; the dearth of substitute teachers if the contracted teacher is unavailable; the need for liability insurance, music royalties, and first aid if someone gets hurt; and the unfortunate break between sessions that occurs just as students are beginning to experience the noticeable benefits of exercising regularly.

Next, we look at the comparative advantages they would gain by working with us. For example, instead of a single hourly teacher with a cluster of supervisory headaches, we provide a certified CPR-trained instructor with a professional substitute backup, her own liability insurance, prepaid music royalties, convenient in-class sign-ups, and ongoing income to the department.

In our experience, the linchpin of negotiations with a bureaucracy is rarely money. Instead, it's the need to permit system flexibility, shift the existing paradigm in order to simplify the administrator's job, and improve the experience of participating customers (both theirs and ours).

If you can present a clear win-win (it must work as well or better for them as it does for you) and remain patient, you can arrive at a successful yes.

UNDERSTANDING THE FLEXIBLE NO

Change is the one constant we can all count on, isn't it? If a situation hasn't changed in a while, rest assured it will. When things are in a state of flux, I hear my mother's voice reminding me, "Keep moving forward, this too shall pass."

The concept of the flexible no accepts that sometimes, at some point in a negotiation, the other party may say, "No," "No, thank you," "Not interested," "Not right for me," "Go away!" As

> *"In business, in many instances, 'no' means 'not right now.'"*
>
> ⸺Jazzercise president
> Shanna Missett Nelson

negative as that sounds and feels, quite often what they're really saying is, "Not right now." "I'm not convinced that what you're offering is right for me." "I'm not in the position to say yes." "I've got too many other things on my plate to deal with you." "Maybe, if you check back later, I'll be able to consider your request."

Kenny Harvey, our vice president of licensing and events, recalls two sterling examples of how, with patience, creativity, and tenacity, a flexible no can be transformed into a successful yes.

Negotiating 201a: Geaux Saints, go!

In 1986, Kenny was a Jazzercise area manager of several deep South states, including Louisiana. Aware that other area managers had generated great enthusiasm, exposure, and additional business by presenting Jazzercise halftime shows for their local NFL teams, Kenny approached Berra Bircher, the then director of entertainment for the New Orleans Saints. "Jazzercisers have delighted NFL crowds in Miami, Dallas, Pittsburgh, San Francisco, and Los Angeles," Kenny told him. "We'd like to provide the Saints with a custom six-minute show, professionally choreographed, performed by 250 to 400 trained dancers on the field in the Superdome . . . at *no cost* to you."

"Such a deal, right?" Kenny says now. "I was certain he'd jump on it; instead, his response was, 'No, thank you, not interested.' I walked away disappointed but resolved to reframe my offer somehow and approach him again the next season."

The following spring, Kenny sent Berra a video highlighting other Jazzercise halftime shows in other NFL stadiums, as well as our featured appearance in the Opening Ceremonies of the Los Angeles Olympics. "Nice," Berra said, "but I don't see it happening in the Superdome."

In year three, Kenny persisted, sending Berra letters of recommendation and commendation from his NFL counterparts in other cities. "Great show," "great organization," "a real crowd-pleaser," the letters said. At their meeting, Berra finally agreed. "Okay, okay, we'll give it a try."

With Berra's yes, we choreographed a six-minute medley of high-energy songs. Next, Kenny and his New Orleans instructors offered their customers a moderately priced performance package that included convenient, in-class practice sessions, dress rehearsal, field admission ticket, a performance costume, box lunch, group photo, and the glory of dancing in the Superdome. Their performance, 400 strong, in the fall of 1989 was terrific, the crowd roared, and the press pronounced it "the best Saints halftime show ever." Kenny reflects proudly, "Berra Bircher was so happy, he invited us back the following year. The 1990 show built to the climax of 'When the Saints Go Marching In' with 750 Jazzercisers spelling out 'Saints' across the football field. The fans went wild."

We later repurposed that show for Jazzercise Japan. At the '91 MYCAL Japan Bowl, an American collegiate all-star football game, in Yokohama, 500 Japanese Jazzercisers participated. That was a performance I'll never forget as I danced my booty off in the freezing cold in white leotard and tights! In '92, 700 Jazzercisers wowed the crowd at the Tokyo Dome by spelling out MYCAL, the sponsor of the game.

None of these extraordinary events would have happened without Kenny's patience, persistence, and creativity in reframing his pitch three different ways, over three years, until the Saints' Berra Bircher finally grasped the win-win.

Negotiating 201b: "Hai" or "lie"?

In the early 1990s, after Kenny's great successes in New Orleans and Tokyo, we tapped him to become head of Jazzercise Japan, our licensed liaison with People Company, a part of that nation's giant MYCAL Group. His job was to explore opportunities to expand the business, and true to form, in four years' time, Kenny did just that—growing Jazzercise Japan, then and now, into our most successful international market.

"Initially, my challenge was understanding the language and the culture," Kenny says. "Especially the fact that, to

Western ears, the Japanese words for 'yes' (*hai*) and 'no' (*iie*) sound very similar. In addition, Japanese culture dictates that one should always strive for harmony and agreement and actively avoid the unpleasantness of disagreement or refusal, i.e., saying no. To a forthright American, this can be very challenging."

In 1992, after getting to know many of our Japanese instructors and students, Kenny approached our partners at People Company for permission to import Jazzercise apparel and other logo items. "Just like in the US, Japanese Jazzercisers are incredibly loyal," he told them. "I am certain they will buy and wear our Jazzercise branded apparel proudly." After much discussion, our Japanese partners politely put him off without a decision.

"It took me months to convince them to say "hai," which was a "yes" to me, so I ordered $15,000 worth of merchandise. Just after it shipped, I advised them it was on its way to Japan and they said they had *not* approved this order. In saying "hai" they were simply saying "We hear you," which to them was not a yes. When I explained to them the order was done, and could not be undone, they said, 'We will not pay for it.' I had no choice but to pay for it myself. They said, 'This merchandise will not sell in Japan; we will lose money.' 'Actually, since I'm the one who paid for it,' I reasoned, 'I'm the one whose money is at risk.' Which turned out to be no risk at all since we sold it all in two weeks!"

"Sometimes, you have to play the long game," Kenny reflects. "Once I was able to demonstrate the strength of the Japanese market, they became and remain a premier customer base for Jazzercise fitness apparel and branded business items." In addition, Jazzercise Japan corporate advisor Tomiko Kagei jokes, "Kenny's efforts in apparel helped launch modeling careers for many of our Jazzercise Japan instructors and staff as they were regularly featured in Jazzercise Apparel catalogs. *Domo arigato*, Kenji-ken!"

It's important to note that international negotiations can be easily derailed if you haven't done your research into cultural nuances and differences. Having a truly bilingual translator is critical, Kenny says, as is attention to local protocols like, in Japan, presenting your business card with two hands instead of one; greeting and treating others with respect, empathy, and humility; and expressing gratitude with an *omiyage* (small, beautifully packaged, edible gift). American companies can have their own cultural protocols as well. If you want to make sure your proposal results in a mutually beneficial agreement, take the time to thoroughly research the organization and the person on the other side. Finding a little common ground can make a surprisingly big difference.

ASK YOUR QUESTION; THE ANSWER MAY SURPRISE YOU

Sandra Langley's experience in New Jersey and Kenny Harvey's in New Orleans and Japan illustrate a Jazzercise maxim: *Ask your question; the answer may surprise you.* If you get a hard yes, congratulations. You've successfully created a winning situation for yourself and the other party.

If you get a flexible no (and we believe that initially all nos are flexible), it's easy to get discouraged, but it's a mistake to just walk away dejected. Instead, rethink your question and their objection, reframe your presentation of your proposal's mutual benefits, then wait a day, a week, a month, or—as in Kenny's case with the New Orleans Saints—a year, then *ask again*. Things change, as do priorities and personnel. It's always worth going back and asking your reframed question again, and perhaps again.

My personal limit is three times: first, to ask my question and listen carefully for any objections I can't immediately answer; second, to ask my reframed question, further discuss the mutually beneficial possibilities, and reveal more of who I am as a potential partner; and third, to lay everything out one last time, affirm my belief in the match, be the patient but persistent squeaky wheel and, hopefully, get the oil.

But don't forget Mary Nuckles MacGyver's dogged pursuit of the producer on "Dinah!" Mary asked, and asked again, a total of *eight* times before successfully scoring the first demonstration of Jazzercise on national television. And that appearance led to invitations to virtually every other major network talk show.

Play the long game patiently, pleasantly, yet persistently. It's worked for us in thousands of negotiations around the planet. And it can work for you to convert that disappointing flexible no into a mutually beneficial yes.

THE MAGICAL POWER OF *WHY NOT?*

Ah, the nineties! In our third decade, 1989 to 1999, Jazzercise continued to grow into a truly global enterprise. Heading into the millennium, we had nearly 5,000 franchisees worldwide, plus multiyear contracts and/or alliances with Nike, General Mills, Mead Johnson, Smuckers, Crystal Geyser, and Ore-Ida potatoes. In line with the technological times, JM Television Productions became JM DigitalWorks and our new website—www.jazzercise.com—vastly improved communications with both our franchisees and our customers. The innovative Jazzercise class locator system enabled anyone globally to access up-to-the-minute info on class locations, formats, days, times, facility amenities, and more.

> *"The common question that gets asked in business is, 'why?' That's a good question, but an equally valid question is, 'why not?'"*
>
> —Amazon CEO Jeff Bezos

The entire decade was not without its bumps, however, as anyone who recalls the 1990–91 Gulf War recession with its spiking oil and gas prices, stock market crash, and ballooning unemployment will affirm. It was during and just after this uncomfortably bumpy ride that I discovered the magical power of "Why not?"

The President's Club: Into the woods, and out again

The impact of the 1990–91 recession on our most produc-tive franchisees—significantly reduced class attendance and income—was painful. Many of them had joined us in the '70s, were aging into their forties and fifties, and though fit, were suddenly talking about retirement. There was increasing chatter about the "good old days" of the '70s and '80s when "all you had to do was post a flyer about a new class and a hundred new customers showed up!" In the throes and after-math of the recession, times were suddenly, uncharacteristi-cally tough and money was tight.

Our regional administrators (upper level management team) were getting an earful in person, and I could read their emailed complaints loud and clear. Effort and enthusiasm among our top producers was flagging. Negativity was ram-pant. My gut was telling me that we needed to *find a way* to turn things around and reenergize them, quick.

To that end, I convened a powwow of top management for a weekend retreat at my cabin in Idyllwild, a small community surrounded by tall pines and fragrant cedars in Southern Cal-ifornia's San Jacinto Mountains. "We *can*, and we *will* figure this out," I told them. "No idea is off the table."

Gathered around the cabin's table, sitting by the fire, shar-ing a walk in the woods, our thoughts were wide-ranging but, to my mind, not immediate enough. After 36 hours of near-constant discussion, most of us arrived at one simple idea. What if we jump-started our franchisees with an incentive plan that supported and rewarded good performers with immediate rebates off their franchise fees?

Margaret Stanton, our always conservative COO, was the lone dissenter. "Why would we do that?"

"Why not?" I asked.

"Well, for starters," she said, "we'd have to invade our reserves."

"What are reserves for if not to help us all get through tough times?" I insisted.

Called the President's Club (because, essentially, I was taking potential profits out of our corporate pocket and putting them back into theirs), the tiered program proved to be a huge and immediate motivator for existing and new franchise owners, who achieved bronze, silver, gold, or platinum performance levels. "The better you perform, the bigger your rebate," I explained. In 1994, the first full year we implemented the program, President's Club rebates totaled $505,197, and sales jumped exponentially. The program proved so popular and productive that, even after things improved, we elected to keep it going. Over the past 25 years, the total amount rebated through the President's Club now exceeds $33 million. Our franchise owners appreciated feeling supported and being rewarded for growing their businesses. And, of course, we appreciated them, since it meant we continued to grow and expand our mission right along with them.

Recessions happen. In tough economic times, it can be tempting to play it safe and question "why?" instead of "why not?" to ideas that involve risk, trusting others, or a leap of faith into new territory. Listen to your gut. Reconnect to the passion and purpose, the drumbeat of belief, that got you here in the first place. If it feels right, go for it.

Jazzercise on Location: "Why not take this show on the road?"

In 1995, after conquering New Orleans and Tokyo, Kenny Harvey came back to our corporate headquarters in Carlsbad, California, to serve as our manager then director of public relations.

Attending one of our quarterly executive meetings, Kenny noted the significant five-times-a-year cost of video-taping newly choreographed routines for distribution every 10 weeks to our franchisees. These updated routines with all-new music and all-new moves are at the core of what keeps Jazzercise current and relevant. And the actual tapings were a popular event among local Jazzercisers and out-of-towners who flew in to vie for dance space in the live class setting.

"It's really a shame that so few people get to attend the tapings," Kenny observed. "What if we took you, the video crew, and the whole show on the road to one of our major markets? It would be fun. And I bet we could mitigate the cost by selling tickets to the event as well as Jazzercise apparel and merchandise on-site."

In Kenny and Margaret's preliminary projections, the numbers were intriguing. In fact, with a full house of paid "dance spaces" plus moderate merchandise sales, there was the possibility that out-of-town tapings might cost out roughly the same as regular tapings in our own Jazzercise studios.

"What do you think?" they asked.

How could I say anything but "Why not?"

Given Kenny's hometown connections in New Orleans, we tried our first "Jazzercise on Location" taping there in September 1997. It was fun, cost effective, and with Kenny's PR efforts, a real shot in the arm to the local market. The following year, we went on location in Europe with great international success in Bern, Switzerland. Our third "Jazzercise on Location" taping was in Chicago, with more than 1,300 enthusiasts attending. Soon, Miami Beach, Baltimore, San Francisco, Austin, and Providence, Rhode Island, followed. In 1999 and into the 2000s, we rebranded these popular events as "Jazzercise Live" with even larger participation in Orlando, Washington, DC, Dallas, Palm Springs, Hiroshima, and many other cities—proof that sometimes "Why not?" is a much better answer than simply "Why?"

Kids Get Fit: Expanding the Great American Fitness Workout

Convinced yet? Here's one more successful "Why not?" idea, which grew out of an invitation for Shanna and me to attend a White House event hosted by President George H. W. Bush and Arnold Schwarzenegger. Called the Great American Fitness Workout, it involved us helping to lead the large crowds gathered on the White House lawn, people of all ages and fitness levels, through a series of exercise routines. We were also there to promote National Fitness Month (traditionally in May) and discuss American children's fitness issues.

Arnold had done his homework. Noting the nationwide

popularity of Jazzercise and citing our unparalleled geographical reach in all 50 states, he challenged us to "do something" to help American kids get fit.

"What could we do?" I wondered on the plane ride home.

"How about a simplified version of Junior Jazzercise presented for free at public schools by volunteer instructors in every Jazzercise market?" Shanna suggested.

"Why not?" I thought.

Called Kids Get Fit, the program was presented to the President's Council on Physical Fitness and Sports the following year and on school playgrounds in all 50 states and internationally throughout the 1990s. By decade's end, more than 1,200 volunteer instructors had engaged more than 2 million kids in free Kids Get Fit classes with the core message that "fitness is for everyone" and "it can be fun!"

In addition to our instructors' efforts at their local schools, we hosted several large Kids Get Fit events in big-city playgrounds in Baltimore, on Chicago's West Side, in south central Los Angeles, and in inner-city San Diego. We ended each event with the song of the decade, "2 Legit 2 Quit," and the kids went wild doing MC Hammer's hand dance on the hook—two fingers up on 2, thumb and index finger forming L for Legit, two fingers up on 2 again, and flat hand wave for Quit. It was every bit as much fun for me as it was for them.

In the end, 2 million kids participated in Kids Get Fit events around the world. Hopefully, they walked away with a different attitude toward exercise and getting fit and realized, maybe for the first time, that fitness could be fun. The idea was good and true; it was philosophically in keeping with our mission; it resonated well with the kids, their teachers, and their parents; it was embraced enthusiastically by our people; and it gave us quality exposure in our communities. Why not, indeed! (There's more on the importance and rewards of community service in Chapter 11, "The Joy of Giving Back.")

CHAPTER 7
CLEF NOTES

♪ Negotiations can be like ballroom dancing. Before you step out on the dance floor, you need to plan some basic moves and project your partner's moves as well. Some dance partners will insist on taking the lead, whereas others will defer to you. Either way, you must pay attention to your partner's cues with the clear aim of getting both of you moving in the same direction.

♪ Warning: Some dance partners don't know they have two left feet. It's up to you to reframe any frustration or misstep into a challenge you *can* resolve. Understand what motivates your partner. Be prepared to offer novel, useful, and clearly mutually beneficial options.

♪ Being rebuffed by someone you're genuinely trying to help is tough. It's tempting to give in to disappointment and simply walk away. Don't do it. Carefully review your first encounter. Be creative in your analysis, wait a while, then go back and try again, and again, until you reach a solution that is a win-win.

♪ Negotiating with others from other cultures requires additional research, empathy, and understanding. Miscommunications happen, even in your native language. Ramp up your creativity, and demonstrate your commitment. If necessary, play the long game. Eventually, it will pay off in more ways than you can imagine.

♪ Peaks and valleys are inevitable, as is the response of some within your company to "wait and see" while potentially golden opportunities and plausible options pass you by. Cue your "gut, head, heart" mantra here. If your gut is telling you something is wrong, listen. Use your head to think through every possible idea or solution. Then follow your heart. Making a decision based solely on the numbers (why?) doesn't always add up. Making decisions based on your mission (why not?) does.

CHAPTER 8

Create a Purposeful Culture

Why are you in business in the first place? The answer to this fundamental question—whether it's to make money, work in a start-up or large corporation, or make a difference in your customers' lives—circumscribes every aspect of your business, workplace, and culture.

A few years back, in his "groundbreaking" management book *Reinventing Organizations*, Belgian author Frederic Laloux proclaimed, "Organizations are moving forward along an evolutionary spectrum, toward self-management, wholeness, and a deeper sense of purpose." Respected scholars, business schools, and consultants all over the world hailed Laloux's book as "a giant leap in management thinking."

My response? Thankfully, we were ahead of this curve 40 years ago.

EGO VERSUS WE-GO

Whether you're in start-up mode or stepping into the leadership role of an existing organization, it's worthwhile to seriously consider your management style. How closely does it reflect your ego and ambitions, your need for control, your ability to trust others? Alternatively, how closely is it aligned with your passion, your values, your purpose and vision for where you and others want to work and what you hope to accomplish?

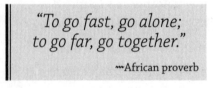

> *"To go fast, go alone; to go far, go together."*
>
> —African proverb

Truly, I've tried it both ways. In the earliest days of Jazzercise, when I was a one-woman show—the boss, bookkeeper, chief teacher, and floor sweeper—I adopted the traditional "command and control" management style. My ego and ambition had me taking on as many classes as I could schedule, my perfectionism dictated every aspect of my class performance, and my lack of trust that anyone else could possibly do what I did pushed my only employee—*me*—to near muteness.

Finally, after eight years of going it alone, losing my voice forced me to train and trust other instructors and to learn how much real pleasure and joy, not to mention greater success, can be achieved by a team—motivated by shared passion and values and committed to tackling challenges together. That insight changed everything.

From the First Ten Jazzercise instructors in 1977 to the 8,500 franchisees we have today, I gave up the top-down "command and control" model and adopted, instead, a policy to "empower and encourage" our people to create and self-manage their own success, come up with their own ideas and run with them, and take responsibility for fixing any missteps or mistakes. Openly and inclusively, results are shared so we can all learn and prosper together. Individual innovations become contributions to the collaborative whole. We actively reinforce them through meaningful recognition and rewards programs.

Although our passion is dance, our deeper purpose is to share the joy, fun, and effectiveness of dance as a fitness regimen, which can and *does* help our customers create healthier, happier lives. To that end, we've built a culture of care: care for oneself, care for others, care for one's community. And we subscribe to our own version of the golden rule: Do unto your people as you would have them do unto your customers.

How do I know the "empower and encourage" approach works? For starters, we've been around five decades, still growing, changing, and innovating. (Ian Davis of *McKinsey Quarterly* wrote, "In a very real sense, survival is the ultimate performance measure.") I'm excited every day to see folks who've been active team members for 10, 20, or as much as 40 years sharing our rich history *and* actively encouraging the fresh new takes and modern perspectives of more recent hires. Each year, we recognize outstanding franchisees for their own success *and* their contributions to the successes of others. Equally important, in a recent survey—2018, our forty-ninth year—we heard it from our customers. When asked to complete the sentence "Jazzercise is _____" with a single word, the most frequent answer, by far, was "Jazzercise is empowering!"

Of course, changing your management style takes more than changing your mind; and creating a culture reflective of your values takes real commitment. Although there's no easy, overnight path, instituting positive, meaningful practices like the ones discussed in this chapter can help.

HIRE FOR ATTITUDE, TRAIN FOR SKILLS

Mary Wadsworth owns and operates two Jazzercise Premier Centers in Houston, Texas. Consistently our top franchisee, Mary has been with us for 35 years and helped select, train, and mentor scores of successful instructors over the years, including her husband, Ken, daughter, Victoria, and son, Marty.

> "*Excellence is not a skill. It's an attitude.*"
> —Writer Ralph Marston

"Securing team members who really care about what they provide makes all the difference," Mary explains. "When asking individuals who are considering becoming a Jazzercise instructor why they are interested in taking the next step, it's great to hear that they love to dance or work out; but it's meaningful when they mention they'd like to help others find answers to their individual challenges—whether it be health, weight loss, increased strength, or getting through a difficult time in their life. Meaningful work with purpose offers value to those on the giving end as well as those receiving."

Stanford University researchers tell us that providing your people with meaningful, purposeful work is important to their well-being and long-term happiness. In addition, they say, purpose has more to do with attitude and approach than with whatever the actual work your company does. Quite often it springs from the live, in-person (non-email, non-text) connections made with others, whether coworkers or customers. Fostering more and better connections among your people is one simple way you can improve your communal sense of purpose. To that end, our instructors often team teach, attend each other's classes as students, and encourage their customers to check out this one's or that one's class in a different yet compatible format. Our customers frequently comment on, and seem to enjoy, the very real camaraderie that exists between fellow instructors.

Another key to fostering more meaningful connections may be to more closely examine your hiring practices.

As a service business, we consciously look for people with a caring attitude, born connectors who are naturally warm, empathetic, and creative. Why? Our customers come to us in all shapes, sizes, fitness levels, and life stages. Our instructors must welcome them warmly, help them feel part of the group, assess their individual needs, and demonstrate any adjustments to help them feel and be successful. In addition to leading the class through 55 carefully choreographed minutes of heart-pumping dance, our instructors must cue the feel and flow of physiologically safe movements and motivate every-one with positive energy and genuine encouragement. These tasks require empathy, creativity, and a sincerely caring at-titude. You can't teach these qualities, but you can recognize and actively recruit candidates who innately possess them.

By the way, the same hiring philosophy applies to our technology department. Our desktop support specialists must be empathetic, able to listen to the issues our internal customers (employees and franchisees) are having, come up with solutions that sometimes require "out of the box" think-ing, and take enough time with each employee to ensure their problem is solved.

Hire for attitude and the innate qualities required to sup-port and accomplish your mission. Everything else can be trained.

SET CLEAR STANDARDS IN TRAINING, PRODUCT AND PROGRAM QUALITY, AND ASSESSMENTS

Once you've attracted the right people, it's critical to provide them with the knowledge, skills, and training they'll need to succeed, and to acculturate them into your way of doing business.

We may have an advantage over other companies, since most of our franchisees are previously committed customers. They've absorbed a lot from their student experience. They live and breathe the passion we all feel. Many see themselves as walking, talking proof that "Jazzercise works," and they want to share that experience with others.

Our training challenge is to move them past the obvious fun, physical, and the-

> *"It's all to do with training; you can do a lot if you're properly trained."*
>
> ~Queen Elizabeth II

atrical aspects of being an instructor—we treat every class as participatory theater of the mind, body, and spirit—and clarify our standards and expectations for all the other aspects of their business.

Our core business is the performance, community, and fitness experience. It requires mastering and teaching updated dance fitness routines to popular music our customers know and love; a working knowledge of the physiology of safe, effective movement; first aid and CPR certification; and the psychology of group leadership, motivation, and relationship building. In addition, there's the discipline required to set goals and persist in achieving them; and the self-control needed to strategically allocate one's attention between learning new routines, preclass practice, professional in-class performance, and outside-of-class marketing, promotion, money management, and team communication.

Because many trainees can feel overwhelmed at first, we've built a team to "encourage and empower" each new franchisee's steps toward success. This is key to any role in any company. Break out what sets you apart, then carefully select and nurture those who join your team. Know specifically what success looks like. Then build a group to support that individual toward that goal.

MODEL CARING, PRIDE, AND GRATITUDE

Not long ago, after working late in my upstairs office, I came down the lobby steps to leave. When I stooped to pick up some dead leaves fallen off an indoor tree, I surprised a new member of our cleaning crew. "Thank you," she said, when I tossed the leaves into the trash can behind our receptionist's desk.

> "It's not fair to ask of others what you are unwilling to do yourself."
>
> ―Eleanor Roosevelt

"Do you teach here?" she asked me.

"Yes, I do."

Then she noticed the similarity between me and the large Jazzercise poster on the wall behind me. "Wait, you're *her?*"

Yep, and I pick up trash, blow up exercise balls, shelve free weights, and generally do whatever else is needed. We all do, and always have. On shipping days five times a year, when we send out our new Choreography Collection (packets containing DVDs of new routines and assorted extras) everyone at Jazzercise headquarters, regardless of level, gets together to stuff, label, and post the 8,500 envelopes bound for our franchisees around the world.

Despite our different roles and responsibilities, we all share the commitment to help each other out when help is needed (and have fun while doing so). I believe that demonstrating that *team means everybody* makes us stronger, more agile, and more connected as a whole.

Whatever your team's size, lead by example, even if that

My first recital, age three

Earning my nickname
"the Upside-Down Girl," age 16

Winning the Most Beautiful Majorette
title with baton fashioned from
ears of corn, 1961

Talent shot for my portfolio and
Gus Giordano Studios,
age 28

My husband, Jack, and me,
Evanston, IL, 1969

My son, Brendan, and me, 1983

Our family:
Shanna, Brendan,
Jack, and me, 1983

My daughter Shanna and
son Brendan, 1993

My parents, June and Del Sheppard, enjoying
strawberries at my fortieth birthday party

*The First Ten Jazzercise instructors
plus a dozen more, 1978*

*The Original Thirty Jazzercise instructors,
plus a few more at Jazzercise Corporate
Office, Carlsbad, California, 1979*

*MCA Gold Record Celebration,
Universal Studios, Los Angeles, 1982*

*The R&B group The Spinners at our first
Jazzercise International Instructors' Convention,
Oceanside, California, 1982*

Dress rehearsal for the Olympics at the Los Angeles Memorial Coliseum, 1984

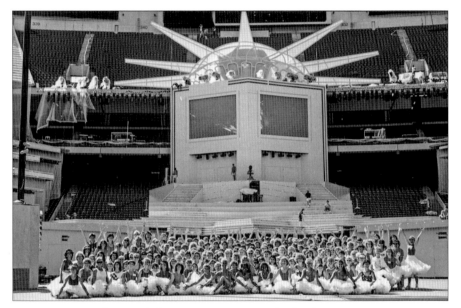

Statue of Liberty rededication ceremony, Meadowlands, New Jersey, 1987

Leading a class at the Jazz Dance World Congress, the Kennedy Center, Washington, DC, 1996

The NBA Pregame Shows for the Houston Rockets, Chicago Bulls, Orlando Magic, Miami Heat, WMBA, and others featured Jazzercise

One of many Jazzercise NFL Halftime Shows, for the Denver Broncos, San Diego Chargers, New Orleans Saints, Kansas City Chiefs, Carolina Panthers, Seattle Seahawks, St. Louis Rams, Detroit Lions, and others

My appearance on the "Gary Collins Hour" TV show, Los Angeles

Dancing at the Great American Workout with First Lady Barbara Bush and Arnold Schwarzenegger, The White House, 1991

On "The Phil Donahue Show," Chicago, 1981

Executive Director John Cates, me, and Jack LaLanne at a California Governor's Council on Physical Fitness and Sports meeting

With Donny Deutsch on "The Big Idea," New York, 2007

"The Pickler & Ben Show," with Emily Newlands Murphy, Kellie Pickler, me, Ben Aaron, and Emily Tyson, Nashville, TN, 2019 (Photo courtesy of "The Pickler & Ben Show." Photo credit: George Burns, Jr.)

My finale class at JazzerJam International Convention,
San Diego, 1995

Thousands attended JazzerJam with premier sponsor Nike,
San Diego, 1995

Jazzercise Dance for Life Breast Cancer Benefit aboard the USS Midway,
San Diego Bay, 2014

Jazzercise warm-up for breast cancer benefit,
Zürich, Switzerland, 2014

Me with daughter Shanna and granddaughters Skyla and Sienna at a corporate photo shoot (Photo courtesy of Lancaster Photographics)

Jazzercise launched GirlForce in 2017, allowing girls aged 16 to 21 to attend classes for free.

Kids Get Fit, a free community outreach program, got kids around the globe moving

The Guinness World Record for largest Junior Jazzercise lesson presented to me, Sienna, Skyla, and Shanna during Jazzercise Live Hiroshima, 2014

CLOCKWISE FROM TOP LEFT:

Gregory Hines, presenter at JazzerJam International Convention, Chicago, 1989

Mikhail Baryshnikov and me at a dance/fitness apparel fashion show in New York, 1990

Shanna and me with "Dancing with the Stars" two-time champion Cheryl Burke, who was also a Jazzercise spokesperson, 2009

My mentor Gus Giordano and Dr. Ruth Westheimer, JazzerJam, Orlando, 1993

Arnold Schwarzenegger, President's Council on Physical Fitness and Sports, Washington, DC, 1992

ABOVE: *MYCAL Japan Bowl Halftime Show, Yokohama, Japan, 1990*

RIGHT: *Me trying to stay warm before the MYCAL Japan Bowl Halftime Show, Yokohama, Japan, 1990*

BELOW: *Jazzercise Japan Rock & Roll Pregame Show for Nippon Ham Baseball, Tokyo Dome, 1991*

Instructor Nancy Brady, me, and granddaughter Skyla taking selfies after the finale class at the Jazzercise Live Hiroshima event with 3,300 attendees, 2014

Visiting the Forbidden City, Beijing, China, 2008

ABOVE, LEFT: *Women Leaders & Global Management Excellence Conference, Beijing, China, 2008.* ABOVE, RIGHT: *Shanna and I presented master classes for Russian fitness instructors and posed in Red Square, Moscow, 1993.* BELOW: *Jazzercise Italy male instructors lead hundreds at Bibione Beach Fitness Convention, 2014*

Receiving the Women Presidents' Organization's
Women's Empowerment Award, 2007

Enterprising Women Hall of
Fame induction for the Lifetime
Achievement Award, 2006

City Sports Magazine *presents Legends Awards to Gilda Marx, Jackie Sorensen,*
Jane Fonda, me, and Jack LaLanne, 1985

Committee of 200, Luminary Award, San Francisco, 2014

Healthy American Fitness Leaders Award, Washington, DC, 1984

When you have been around as long as I have, I think you get lucky and people give you awards. I'm very humbled and grateful for all this recognition.

Just us girls: Sienna, Shanna, me, and Skyla, 2017

*Hanging out after class, Carlsbad, California, 2018
(Photo courtesy of Lancaster Photographics)*

*My granddaughters Skyla and Sienna and me getting our kicks out of dancing
(Photo courtesy of Lancaster Photographics)*

means wiping down counters or taking out trash. Model your values. Help others connect to them and to you. I can affirm, without question, that your company will be stronger and last longer if you do.

PROMOTE TRUST THROUGH TRANSPARENCY

Four times a year, we hold our all-hands-on-deck quarterly meetings. That means hiring temps to answer the phones so our receptionist and customer care employees can attend. Those who are local join us in person. Those who are remote are encouraged to attend electronically via GoToMeeting. This is when we welcome new employees, celebrate anniversaries, announce awards to thank those who've gone above and beyond, and share time with each other.

> "Honesty is the first chapter in the book of wisdom."
> —Thomas Jefferson

You get what you give. Caring is a two-way street, as is pride in what we do and why and how we do it; gratitude for those who share our passion and our purpose; trust that we have each other's backs and—always, always—complete transparency. Everything, even our most proprietary plans and projects, is openly discussed.

At Jazzercise, openness is not just a goal, it's an operating principle, which is why we have very few doors in our corporate headquarters and no barriers to constructive feedback and communication from the field. Before we implement any significant program, update, or change, we communicate the what, why, and how first. People respond better when they understand your point of view and can see that the goal is a winning situation for everyone.

One example of our openness-in-all-things policy occurred relatively recently. After dismissing our director of finance in 2014, we carefully confirmed that she had been embezzling significant amounts of money, over many years, from both the corporate and Jack's and my personal bank accounts. Prior to her arrest in early 2017, and the potential of the press taking a private situation public, I felt it critical to explain, via video message to all our franchisees, the situation and our actions taken. I also felt it was important to provide my personal guarantee that this unfortunate incident would in no way impact them, our planned programs, or the overall health of the company. When the story came out, instructors were informed and prepared to reassure their customers that, regardless of the potentially glaring headlines that could come, all was good. As it turned out, the coverage was matter-of-fact, mostly local, and thankfully without much fanfare. It could have gone either way. Collectively, we were ready.

SYNCHRONIZE YOUR SYSTEMS—PEOPLE, PRODUCTS, PROGRAMS—TO REFLECT YOUR VALUES

If your values are clear to you and to everyone on your team, if it's accepted that all actions must be in tune with those

> "The quality of a leader is reflected in the standards they set for themselves."
>
> ⸺Businessman Ray Kroc

values, you greatly improve the chances of a desirable and harmonious outcome. Here's one example of how this works for us.

There is no substitute for top quality. We value and take great pride in the quality of our people, our programs for our franchisees and customers, and in every performance attached to Jazzercise, whether it's a daily class, a demo at a local mall, or an NFL halftime show.

Our satellite sales manager, Joan Missett Gambill, and her sister, executive advisor Kathy Missett, grew up immersed in "the Jazzercise way." Their mother, my sister-in-law Sandra Missett, was my invaluable executive assistant for 35 years. In a recent email, Joan explained how and why our belief in top quality permeates everything we do: "Judi never settles for less, and neither can we. Be it a convention setting where she wants it to be the best, or with every program we put in place, she does it top notch. Price is not a factor in these decisions, as she knows, in the long run, quality in all you do will pay off."

Kathy, my MBA niece, added, "We make decisions based on what is right, not necessarily nor solely on what it costs. So, dollars and sense."

Commitment to quality runs through every aspect of our business: from the exceptional feel and flow of our classes, to the design and durability of our apparel, to the polish of our public performances. People notice, and our efforts are rewarded in innumerable ways. After our Opening Ceremonies performance at the LA Olympics, for example, famous film and television producer David Wolper called to invite us to join the nationally televised rededication of the Statue of Liberty celebration. That show, that exposure was a real thrill (and a PR boon) for us. As was David's note later saying, "Every part of the celebration that you helped make possible with the Statue of Liberty Jazzercise group was first-class. I feel honored to have worked with you."

Whatever values you as team leader establish up front will directly impact what comes out in the end. The clearer and more consistent you are in connecting others to the same principle, the more certain you can be of the outcome.

PRACTICE, PRACTICE, PRACTICE: WHY REHEARSAL, A THEATRICAL EXPERIENCE, AND CONTINUED TRAINING ARE IMPORTANT TO US

My early years as a professional dancer and theatrical performer taught me the importance of rehearsal. Performance without adequate preparation is rarely first rate. It takes practice to get it right.

For this reason, our instructors practice and prepare for each class ahead of time so that the individual and group experience during class is unmarred by

> *"We learn by practice. Whether it means to learn to dance by practicing dance or to learn to live by practicing living, the principles are the same."*
> ⸺Dance icon Martha Graham

fumbling for notes, searching for music, adjusting lights, correcting sightlines, or any other distracting mishaps.

In addition to individual strength and fitness, many studies show that dance improves the alignment of one's thoughts, behavior, and emotions; and group dance led by a qualified instructor fosters a deeper connection with oneself and others, as well as the ability to create, innovate, build rapport, foster trust, and increase self-confidence. We have known for years that the special alchemy of upbeat music, group dance, peaking heart rates, and the resulting flow of energy, sweat, and endorphins is what sets Jazzercise apart from every other fitness option, generates the most loyal following, and produces the largest, longest retention of customers in the industry.

Outside our classes, practice is equally important in demonstrating the Jazzercise experience to others. We take pride in the fact that our public performances are as polished as any professional dance troupe out there. From the White House to Lincoln Center, the Olympics to the Super Bowl, the Statue of Liberty to the flight deck of the USS *Midway* aircraft carrier in San Diego Bay, we *know* how to put on a great show! Our secret: passion, commitment to quality, and as much practice as it takes to get it right.

Joan Missett Gambill explains: "While I've been victim of many long, brutal rehearsals, Judi's standards always shine through. We will practice until it is perfect so that nothing but the best is seen. From international conventions in Italy and Japan (which I had the honor of being a part of) to a demo at a street fair, everything we put out there will always be professional. Once, when we were at a convention in Italy, Judi, Shanna, and I were practicing in the green room. Judi had just taught and performed but wanted us to be perfect for the on-site taping of new routines. She sat down and started practicing in her chair. We had to laugh because she fell asleep in the chair practicing—but this is a snapshot of how she never quits where quality is concerned!"

Be a stickler for your standards. If you don't quit, your people won't either.

BRING EVERYONE TOGETHER

Our people work hard. In any given week, they're teaching 32,000 classes per week, inspiring roughly 70,000 customers every day. They care about each of their customers, as we care about each of our instructors. Which is why we frequently get together at regional and global Jazzercise conferences to connect,

> *"If everyone is moving forward together, then success takes care of itself."*
>
> ---Henry Ford

dance, celebrate, learn from each other, and have fun. Having fun together has always been, and always will be, a core value.

In 2017, we launched The Studio, our interactive learning management system (LMS), to significantly upgrade our worldwide exchange of info, ideas, support, and training. In a single year, we achieved 98 percent usage by our franchisees, sharing hundreds of thousands of messages with each other. Ironically, the success of our then 48-year-old company's LMS earned our platform supplier a Rookie of the Year award for outstanding design, engagement, vitality, and community.

Why wasn't I surprised? At Jazzercise, we've always made time for and prized getting everyone together—whether in person, by live-streaming, or in our online Studio exchange. The *esprit de corps* established by the First Ten instructors has been successfully scaled across many thousands and multiple platforms. We wouldn't be Jazzercise without it.

Think of your passion and values as the through-line, the spine of your company story. Clarify them, communicate them, build your culture around them, encourage your people to embrace them, and empower individuals to act on them. If you're not doing this already, try it. I'm certain you'll see and appreciate the difference.

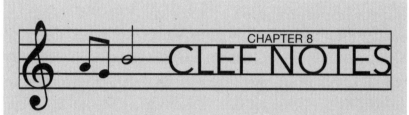

CHAPTER 8

CLEF NOTES

♪ What are the values in your company's culture that circumscribe who you are? Are they clear to everyone, consistently communicated, consciously adhered to in all your team does? At the end of the day, do they provide everyone involved with a sense of meaning and purpose?

♪ When interviewing candidates, truly listen to what the people sitting across from you are saying. What experiences and challenges have shaped them? How did they learn and grow? Where are they now and where do they want to be? What interests and excites them about your mission? Does their passion, personal attitude, and innate qualities align with your company's? They may be amazingly talented and charismatic, but if their passion is elsewhere, eventually they will be elsewhere, too.

♪ Speaking of alignment, insist that every aspect of your organization—from people to production, finance to technology, training to assessments—reflects your culture's standards and values. As the leader, model the behaviors you expect from others. If caring, high quality, and hard work are important to your organization, show your team your commitment to those values. Be purposeful and diligent in tending your culture by keeping standards in place.

♪ As team members and, essentially, as humans, we love to connect. And as any anthropologist will tell you, it starts with the eyes. If you're the owner, founder, CEO, president, or head of your organization, get out of your office and connect with your teams. Look them in the eyes, take time, show interest, get to know them, and let them get to know you. Share a moment or a meal or an all-hands project with them.

♪ Make connecting and transparently communicating an integral part of your culture. Bring everyone together on a regular basis, face to face or through digital channels, to discuss your challenges, mark your milestones, and celebrate your communal successes.

CHAPTER 9

Cultivate Your Customer Community

Who is your audience? What do you offer them that no one else does? How can you guarantee they'll come back to you, again and again?

Judi

Among businesspeople, there's unending talk and advice about customers: how to identify them, attract them, keep them, and, in today's world, make sure they engage with you heavily on social media *and* recommend you to their friends.

The rules of customer engagement have greatly expanded, beyond old-school "customer service," which was often a euphemism for the complaint department, a place to send customers unhappy with a product or service. Today, more companies promote their "customer care," which is a higher level of interaction designed to discern what the customer genuinely wants or needs and provide them with the appropriate solution. (Think of that scene in the classic film *Miracle on 34th Street*: "Macy's doesn't carry the skates you need, but Gimbel's does!")

More recently, the buzz is all about "customer experience," which, in March 2018, *Forbes* magazine defined as "the sum of all contact" your customer has with your company; "the emotional, physical, and psychological connections customers have with a brand." It's not a one-time, drive-through interaction, but a customer's entire life cycle with your brand, including every contact he or she has with your people, products, or services.

Now we're getting somewhere. According to *Forrester's Customer Experience Index* (CX Index), publicly traded companies with higher CX Index rankings routinely enjoy higher stock price growth and higher total returns. In other words, providing your customers with the best possible experience, long term and on multiple levels, is both popular with your customers *and* great for your business.

It's certainly been great on every level for Jazzercise.

PEOPLE DON'T CARE TO KNOW UNTIL THEY KNOW YOU CARE

I love this quote from Louis Armstrong. It not only explains why Satchmo was one of the most beloved and influential

> *"The main thing is to live for that audience, 'cause what you're there for is to please the people!"*
>
> ⸺Louis Armstrong

figures in jazz history, it also nails the idea of being customer-centric. The term *customer-centric* means putting your customers at the center or heart of everything you do, remembering as Joan Leavitt, my first dance instructor, liked to say, "The audience always counts."

When, in 1969, I attempted to teach professional jazz dance techniques to a class of neighborhood and studio moms, and 90 percent of them dropped out, I learned Joan's lesson the hard way. But I've never forgotten it since.

Jazzercise was born customer-centric, in the moments I asked my dropouts what they were looking for, invited them back, turned them away from the mirror, and encouraged them to enjoy the music, follow me the best they could, have fun and, over time, achieve the fitness, tone, smaller dress size, and physical and emotional well-being they craved.

In today's vernacular, each of these actions was a "touchpoint," a single interaction that, one by one, added up to each customer's total experience, or "journey." Do you know how many touchpoints are involved in your customers' overall experience with your business? Do you care about what the total "journey" of doing business with you is like, start to finish, from your customers' point of view?

We do, because we ask, we observe, we actively work to make each customer's Jazzercise journey the best it can be. And we're rewarded by the highest customer loyalty and retention levels in the fitness industry.

How do we do it? There's no single or easy answer. Providing great customer experience is the sum of many different, often challenging parts—the first of which is a firm, clear commitment on your part, and by that I mean from the top down, that delivering the best possible customer experience is critical to your growth and value.

CREATE A CUSTOMER COMFORT ZONE

These days, customers have more choices than ever. They shop for everything, from phones to fashion, cars to backpacks, food to fitness options. Frequently, their choice can be more emotional than financial. If your goal is to grab their attention and convert them to loyal, long-term customers, my strong suggestion is to put yourself in their place and, step by step,

> *"You never get a second chance to make a first impression."*
>
> ⸺Actor Will Rogers

make them feel "you are welcome here, we have what you're looking for, and we're going to make it easy and enjoyable for you to get what you want for as long as you want it."

Here's how Elizabeth West, our satellite sales manager for 18 central states, explains it: "The scariest thing is to walk through the door of your first class. You feel out of shape, alone, and nervous. We go out of our way to welcome you. We lead with names, we introduce you to others, and we make sure your first class is a positive one."

Kelly Sweeney, our chief sales and marketing officer, adds: "We've always positioned ourselves as the 'everyperson's workout program.' To deliver on that promise, we select instructors who can naturally create a welcoming and comfortable environment, more personable and less intimidating than most gyms or higher-priced boutique fitness options. At the same time, we rigorously train our instructors to listen carefully and quickly assess each person's goals and needs. We spell out and cue specific modifications and safe alternatives for movement. We want each customer to feel success—no matter where they are on the fitness spectrum—and to make the workout truly 'work' for them."

Our combination of clear values, quality hiring practices, and extensive skill training works for *us* to establish up front a strong individual customer relationship and, longer term, a loyal, supportive community. Each part is integral to the whole.

What are the parts of your company that combine to create a comfort zone for your customer? Are you confident that a new customer's initial touchpoint with your brand (in all ways, whether that means on the phone or over the Internet, walking through the door, or at your sales or ticket counter) will yield a positive first impression? Do you have standards in place to guarantee that their subsequent encounters will be equally positive and comfort producing? Is your goal to transform each customer into a member of your brand-loyal community? If not, it should be.

GOOD MANNERS COUNT

My midwestern parents had no patience with bad manners; neither do I, nor will your customers. Good manners—getting to know people's names, being a good host, nurturing others, making sure everyone is getting what they came for—are not optional; they're essential to the Jazzercise experience. It's the first and foremost way we show our customers that we care about them.

> "Good manners reflect something from inside— an innate sense of consideration for others and respect for self."
>
> ⸺Emily Post

In this, as my parents did for me, I choose to lead by example. Most people want to be seen, supported, and appreciated. Whether interacting with customers or employees, I instill a personal touch by remembering a person's name, sending a note of thanks or a gift, taking the time to call, or providing appreciation in person. These may seem like small things, but they can mean a lot to the person receiving them.

"We actually spend time on this in every instructor training and all sales meetings," Kelly Sweeney says. "Good manners are a huge part of who we are. It's a core value at Jazzercise, so we make it important and support it with tools, training, and assets."

Obviously, good manners involve much more than a sincere "please" and "thank you." They also extend to listening without interruption, expressing empathy and understanding over someone's upset, genuinely apologizing, and taking real and rapid action to resolve an issue.

You get what you give, right? Because they know we care about them, our customers care about us. Seventy percent of them care enough to recommend us to a friend, colleague, or family member.

Want to know if your customers feel truly cared for and are caring in return? It's all there in your accumulation, conversion, retention, and referral rates, as well as your online and real-time word-of-mouth. Got a problem? Insisting on top-to-bottom good manners—*no matter what*—may be a simple but excellent place to start.

MILESTONES MATTER

Our policy on milestones is simple: Remember them, recognize them, and celebrate them. It shows your customers (and your team members) you notice, you care, and the relationship you share is meaningful.

> *"Remember to celebrate milestones as you prepare for the road ahead."*
>
> ---Nelson Mandela

Because we're in the fitness business, we're here to help our customers get fit. In the simplest of terms, the more they show up, the faster we'll both achieve and maintain their fitness objectives. Why wouldn't we encourage, celebrate, and reward them for all the hard work? Unlike some fitness programs, which often seem more interested in signing clients up for auto-pay than in actually seeing them show up, we call, send cards, drop emails to let our customers know we've missed them and to tell them that we hope to see them soon.

Our belief is when customers have invested in us, we invest in them. We want to be as much a partner in their success as they are in ours.

I've asked Kelly, our chief sales and marketing officer, to explain a bit more. Perhaps it will trigger some thoughts and ideas as to how a milestone program might work for your business.

"I've attended fitness programs all over the country for more than 30 years. I've never seen nor heard any of them recognize attendance. It's simple, but not often done. We train our people on milestones, ongoing. We support them with materials—postcards, messaging, and email templates—and with in-class promotions that recognize and celebrate current customers for either attendance or for sharing/referring the program to others." In fact, word-of-mouth and friend-to-friend referrals account for well over two-thirds of our new customers.

Kelly continues, "From the beginning, Judi made celebrations a part of what we do. We spend time and money on remembering, recognizing, and rewarding customer milestones. We do it a lot and we do it well. For example, customers who attend 150 classes in a calendar year achieve Club Jazzercise status, recognition, and rewards. Other programs include our Summer Attendance games and prizes, February Fitness Challenge, and Bring a Friend recognition and rewards held at various times throughout the year. Although we plan and prepare support items at corporate, these popular programs are things our franchisees and customers *love* and quickly adopt and embrace."

In addition to attendance milestones, we also remember and celebrate birthdays, holidays, and big anniversaries in class. In support of our earliest customer promise—fitness, friendship, and fun—celebrations help fuel the fun and add strength and endurance to our customer relationships.

By the way, while our franchisees monitor and remember milestones for their customers, we do the same thing for our franchisees and employees, celebrating work anniversaries, birthdays, and other significant life events. Recently, for example, Elizabeth West reached her twenty-fifth year as a Jazzercise manager. To show my appreciation to all our US sales managers, I hosted their team meeting at my home and recognized Elizabeth in front of her peers with both praise and a personalized gift and card.

Elizabeth wrote, "Throughout my Jazzercise career I have received countless awards and recognition, each time more special than the last because I know it comes from the heart."

I wholeheartedly agree with Sir Richard Branson, founder of Virgin Group, who says, "The way you treat your employees is the way they will treat your customers. People flourish when they are praised."

Recognize and appreciate your customers' achievements and your team members' contributions. A small but sincere act of acknowledgment can motivate, encourage, or inspire, ease a burden, boost confidence, or simply warm the other person's heart. Our objective for each and every Jazzercise class or encounter is to make the other person feel better for having been there. What's yours?

FOSTER CONNECTIONS THAT CONTINUE BEYOND YOUR WORKPLACE

> *"It's actually because you're in their lives, because you've created something for them, that they are there showing up—because of you, and because of the community you've built around them, and because of the way you make them feel."*
>
> ⁓TV's "Biggest Loser" trainer Jennifer Widerstrom addressing the 2018 Jazzercise Franchisee Conference in Nashville

All the actions mentioned in Jennifer's comment create connections and continuity between our instructors and their customers and among our customers themselves. Our "we welcome all" and "fitness and fun for everyone" culture means we host our class as a party; we learn each other's names; we recognize and celebrate each person's hard work and accomplishments. Over time, fellow students who may have nothing in common except Jazzercise become friends. They often meet after class for coffee, read books, attend theater, and plan holiday celebrations together.

Longtime Jazzercise instructor Nancy Brady said recently, "We experience *life* together, via a fitness program that is way more than just a workout. We've gone through marriages, divorces, births, deaths, cancers, autism, and losing weight together. The workout is the foundation of how we all met, but the relationships we've made while doing the workout is what makes us a family."

Jenet Morrison, another veteran instructor, added, "Coming together is a dynamic you see in Jazzercise between instructors and customers, instructors and instructors, and customers and customers, and it's what makes us unique. I believe that Judi's philosophy of keeping the personal touches in Jazzercise—like announcing class milestones, greeting customers by name, singing 'Happy Birthday' in class, and sending handwritten cards—is so important! Those small things add up to mean a lot to our customers and keep them feeling valued when they may not get that feeling from any other area in their lives."

Mindy Batt, a valued customer of 24 years, explains it this way: "I'm grateful every day to have found something that I love so much, that benefits me not only physically but also mentally and socially. I can't imagine my world without Jazzercise in it."

While anecdotal quotes from instructors and customers are wonderful, our industry-leading stats should convince you how important—imperative, even—it is to connect with your customers: 50 percent of our customers have been attending Jazzercise for 10 years or more, compared to only 15 percent of the general health club population. Further, 68 percent participate in Jazzercise classes more than three times a week, compared to only 44 percent of the general health club population.

If you want to create and hold on to a vibrant, long-lasting customer community, connect and commit to keeping them at the heart of everything you do. The returns will be both measurable and, at the same time, incalculable.

TRUST YOUR CUSTOMERS TO DO THE RIGHT THING? WE DO!

I believe that how you choose to run your company, treat your employees, and interact with your customers has a lot to do with your worldview.

In fact, isn't the desire to do things our way, to prescribe our vision and hoped-for version of things the key reason most entrepreneurs start our own business in the first place?

> *"I'm not much on gimmicks. I never have been because they don't last."*
>
> —Jazz singer and bandleader Billy Eckstine

In my worldview, the vast majority of people give what they get. Treat them with genuine care, real respect, trust, and transparency and they will do the same to you. My extensive experience—assuming one considers five decades extensive—has proven this true time and time again.

To me, trust is the bedrock upon which all relationships, business or otherwise, are built. And while it takes time to build trust—through competence, reliability, integrity, and open communication—trust can also be destroyed quite quickly.

As CEO, you will often be called on to make decisions seemingly unrelated to customer or employee trust. A program meant to improve operational efficiencies, for example, or to streamline processes for greater profitability can seem like a no-brainer. But if, down the line, the result decreases the quality of your customers' experience, creates frustrating time delays, involves onerous paperwork, or makes them feel untrusted, uncared for, or unconsidered, that no-brainer decision can quickly become a huge headache and trust-buster.

Our core values of trust and transparency underpin everything we do. Unlike others in the fitness industry, we apply it to our contracts, which are open-ended and time tiered yet easily canceled or put on hold at any time. We also apply it to our apparel sales, including the often-frenzied apparel try-ons and sales at our customer-included conventions.

We trust our customers to do the right thing, and the overwhelming majority of them do. (The very small percentage who don't rarely hang around for long.) We don't play games with pricing, we don't use gimmicks to gain commitments, and we don't ruin anyone's credit because they're locked into an iron-clad, small-print contract.

We play it straight. We don't expect abuse and, by and large, we rarely experience it. To me, honesty and forthrightness is a worldview, trust and transparency are core values, and almost all customers will sense and respond in an appropriate and like manner.

Call me overly optimistic, naïve, old-fashioned, anything you wish, but, unapologetically, gaining trust by giving it works for us. It always has been and always will be a critical component in our delivery of the completely customer-centric Jazzercise experience.

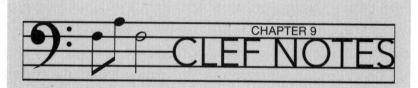

CHAPTER 9
CLEF NOTES

♪ Have you done all you can to make your business customer-centric?

♪ Long-term research by *Forrester's Customer Experience Index* proves that higher business valuations go hand in hand with happier customers. Why not examine each of the touchpoints your customers experience with your brand, product, or service? Study how you can improve each interaction to demonstrate that their comfort and satisfaction is important to you and that you value their support.

♪ Whether you're dealing with customers, employees, franchisees, vendors, or clients, never underestimate the value of little things like good manners, acknowledging achievements, remembering milestones, and recognizing contributions. It's human nature to crave recognition, support, and sincere appreciation. Strive to provide that, to make each person feel a part of a caring community, and watch your word-of-mouth, positive online reviews, and referral rates soar.

♪ As CEO, take the time to examine your worldview, as it may influence, expand, or limit every decision you make on behalf of your company and all involved in your enterprise. You're not just the boss, you're the head of a community in need of your care. It may be easy to earn their trust initially, but it's hard work to consider and maintain their trust over the long haul. That trust, however, is *crucial* to your success. To that end, evaluate every product, service, policy, or procedure in terms of its end result: will it build personal and/or communal trust or bust it?

♪ Even if you're running a highly profitable Internet-based business out of your garage, selling products or services to people you'll never meet or see, the importance of trust and transparency remains the same. Never lose sight of the real live person on the other end of the transaction—who has selected your offering to ease, improve, or enrich their journey. Honor their leap of faith in choosing you over so many other options and deliver, simply and transparently, on the trust they've extended to you.

CHAPTER 10

Assessing Expectations, Maintaining Excellence

My twist on the old adage "inspect what you expect" is to inspect what my people need, individually and as a team, in order to create the results I expect from them.

Judi

Creating a purposeful culture for your people and a supportive community for your customers is important. But wishing won't make it so. Equally important is clearly communicating your mission, values, and specific expectations and conducting regular assessments to determine and close the gaps between your expectations and the day-to-day reality taking place in the field.

Of course, assessments come in many forms. One option is to disguise yourself and observe your team anonymously, as many CEOs have done on the popular TV show "Undercover Boss." Another option is to study "the metrics," track and analyze each measurable data point in your business. At Jazzercise, we track each instructor's customer accumulation, conversion, and retention rates. We also regularly survey our customers' satisfaction levels and monitor all reviews and comments on social media.

But, to me, the shortest, fastest, most effective route is to personally and regularly connect with each person, show a genuine interest in what's working and what isn't for them, analyze whether the issue is isolated or widespread, then provide meaningful support to bring their performance to expected levels. With a workforce of 8,500 franchisees teaching 32,000 classes per week in all 50 states plus 25 foreign countries, how do we do it?

CLOSING THE GAP BETWEEN EXPECTATIONS AND REALITY

Hiring the right person for the job is just the beginning. No matter how detailed, organized, or complete a new hire's original training, over time you'll find that gaps will surface between your original expectations and their ongoing in-field execution. Call it human nature, enterprising individualization, whatever. It happens. So, if quality control and consistent excellence is important to you, you must have a plan to continually close the gap. Here's ours:

> *"Don't expect what you don't inspect."*
>
> ⁓Businessman and writer
> W. Clement Stone

1. **Clearly define your expectations.** Does each of your team members understand the core competencies required and expected (the how and the why) to perform his or her role in your collective mission? For instance, each Jazzercise instructor is expected to demonstrate three core competencies, which range from appropriate physical movements to safe and engaging instructional performance to sound class set structures based on proven fitness principles.

2. **Lead with self-assessment.** If your expectations are clear, individuals should be given the opportunity to assess themselves and determine areas of strength or need for improvement. At Jazzercise, we regularly request that all instructors record themselves leading a 55-minute class and then evaluate their performance against a one-page core competencies/key skills checklist. At this point, they have the opportunity to self-correct and rerecord, or to submit their initial recording as is and request help in self-prescribed areas.

3. Follow with formal review and assessment.
A one-on-one evaluation should aim to clear up any misunderstandings of the core competencies or performance levels expected. Our individual assessment coordinators review each instructor's submitted recording within two weeks of submission, then, via frequent Skype check-ins, assume the role of personal trainer/coach to correct individual issues.

4. Follow up with coached corrections, then reassess. Repeat regularly. Any required corrections should be personally and thoroughly discussed to assure complete understanding and agreement. Change must be motivated and supported with respect, patience, and encouragement. Our assessment coordinators provide one-on-one coaching to our instructors with the aim of helping them reach a new, more successful level of teaching through the experience.

Different companies have different attitudes toward regular assessments. What's yours? When your team is small, assessments and corrections often happen naturally through close observation and personal feedback. But when you grow and spread across different facilities and locations, it's a mistake to assume that singular processes covered in new-hire training will be followed without fail in the field, even by seasoned supervisors. Some may see the assessment process as an unnecessary expense or "necessary evil." That's a mistake, too. My strong advice is to recast it as a very practical way to clarify expectations, positively promote consistent performance, thoughtfully support personal progress, and ensure the success of both the individual and the overall team. It's a lot harder than donning an undercover wig or a fake mustache but, in our experience, infinitely more effective.

IDENTIFY AND EXEMPLIFY OUTSTANDING TEAM MEMBERS

> *"A good example has twice the value of good advice."*
>
> ---Albert Schweitzer, winner of the Nobel Peace Prize

Most managers have no problem identifying their exemplary team members. They're the ones you feel lucky to have and wish you could clone. They not only meet your expectations, but routinely exceed them, and they often win their team's performance and incentive awards. Although you may consider these individuals a valuable sales or production asset, don't overlook their additional value as an example and inspiration to their fellow teammates.

Take Toni Pitruzzello, for instance. Toni is an outstanding Jazzercise instructor who, throughout her eight-year career with us, has accumulated a fanatically loyal following among her ever-increasing customer base. Her classes are routinely packed, and her energy, excitement, and customer conversion rates are exceptional. Would I clone Toni if I could? You bet! Instead, we did the next best thing.

We approached Toni to teach a four-part presentation, called "How to Be an Amazing Associate," on The Studio, our online, interactive LMS. Her objective, we explained, was not professional training, but confessional sharing of her secrets, instructor to instructor, with the same empathy and connectivity she uses with customers in her classes. To that end, Toni put together a terrific and very popular series demonstrating how she "ups her game" on a regular basis and how other instructors can do the same. Using examples from her own "day in the life of a Jazzercise instructor," she provided a treasure trove of valuable ideas, experiences, and suggestions for her peers.

In the example that follows, in which Toni walks her fellow instructors through her step-by-step process of new-customer conversion, you can feel the energy, intelligence, and beating heart of a top performer at work.

Arrive early. "I always arrive early to class," Toni explains. "This allows me to gauge my customers' preclass mood and energy level and begin to either harness it or elevate it to create 'good mojo' from the get-go." Whatever the event—a class, interview, sales appointment, or presentation—Toni's point is that arriving early can provide valuable intel from others—the company receptionist, your prospect's secretary, or other meeting attendees—that helps you customize your behavior to the task at hand.

Chat with prospects before class. Toni's excellent advice is to "introduce yourself, note names, and ask a few open-ended questions like 'What are you looking for in an exercise program?' 'Who brought you in today? How do you know each other?' Then subtly prepitch your offering." The personal prepitch prior to an actual class, meeting, or presentation gives your prospect time to think, analyze, and evaluate why they're here. It also gives them the opportunity to ask a question or two and reveal any private concerns.

Teach a stellar class. "I teach a stellar class, having so thoroughly practiced and prepared that everything I say or do appears effortless. Proper preparation enables me to shift the focus away from what I'm doing and onto how my customers are responding." Here Toni's point is, regardless of the sales or service situation, if you've prepared well enough in advance to put yourself at ease, you'll be able to put your customer at ease as well, and you will have a much clearer understanding of whether they are agreeing with and/or accepting your material. This enables you to adjust your pitch accordingly.

Get off the stage *fast*. "After class, I get to the door as quickly as I can to say good-bye to my existing customers and to catch the newcomers before they leave. This is where the magic happens," Toni says. In any presentation or sales situation, it's important to definitively wrap up the nonpitch portion of your exchange and move quickly to the meat of the matter.

Ask your question. Toni's strong suggestion is to "lead with gratitude and a sincere compliment—for example, 'Thanks so much for coming. You did *so* well and looked like you had so much fun!'—then move quickly to the critical question. 'You said earlier you're ready to get serious about your fitness and we're here to help you do it. In fact, you've come at the perfect time because we have this special [insert current promo]. May I tell you about it?'" At Jazzercise, we never practice high-pressure or bait-and-switch or any other less than win-win tactic. Instead, we strongly advocate, "Just ask your question and listen carefully for their response. If they say yes, great. If they say no, thank them and invite them back to another class." The same technique applies to a more formal business or sales setting. Ask your question and pay careful attention to the reply. And don't forget that, in most cases, *no* means "not right now."

Don't kick yourself. "If your prospect is not ready to sign up, should you kick yourself over a lost conversion? *Absolutely not!*" Toni says. "At Jazzercise, we have such an awesome program that two out of every three visitors return to become regular customers. An initial no only brings you closer to their eventual yes!" Excellent advice, I'd say. If you've carefully prepared and practiced your pitch, delivered it professionally, and still gotten a no, it's time to consider the long game. Reframe your approach, highlight new win-win benefits, and, after a time, ask again. If need be, ask again after that.

How many Toni Pitruzzellos are working in your business and keeping their awesome award-winning secrets to themselves? Can you reenvision your top performers as an invaluable in-house resource? Why not invite them to share their expertise and provide knowledgeable insider inspiration to their fellow teammates?

ASSESSING YOUR CUSTOMERS' SATISFACTION LEVELS

Of course we assess our customers' satisfaction levels, don't you? But how? Formal surveys tend to reveal valuable trends and insights. The word cloud in Figure 10.1, for example, shows the words our customers mention when asked what they like best about Jazzercise. The larger the word, the more often it was mentioned.

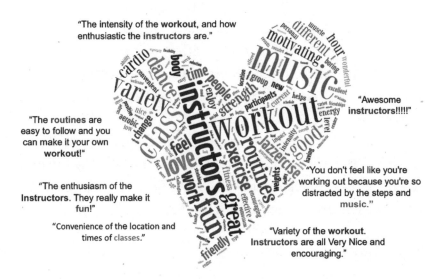

FIGURE 10.1. What customers like about Jazzercise

I enjoy seeing the results of our quantitative customer surveys. But, as with teammate assessments, my preference is to personally and regularly connect with a wide variety of customers to gain a more in-depth understanding of what's working for them, what's not, and why. As CEO, you need and want to know: Are we providing the best possible customer experience on multiple levels? Which touchpoints with our brand are working well? Where are the pain points? How can we improve in order to accomplish our mission?

> *"We all need people who will give us feedback. That's how we improve."*
>
> ---Bill Gates

Again, my advice to you is to get out there and personally connect with your customers on a regular basis. One of our mantras is "Ask your question; the answer may surprise you." Each week, I teach three Jazzercise classes and attend two to three others. I take those opportunities to ask open-ended questions of a wide range of our customers. Do you have a list of questions you use to connect with your customer community? You probably should. There's just no substitute for making a one-on-one, heart-to-heart connection with members of your core audience.

In the following pages I provide the five questions I routinely ask my customers, the information I'm looking for, and the responses I have received. Maybe they will inspire you to get out there and do something similar.

Question 1: What brought you to Jazzercise, and why have you remained a loyal customer?

What I'm really asking: Which of our promotions worked to get you through the door? What's the significant touchpoint that helped you to commit? Are you getting what you came for? How exactly are we fulfilling your needs and expectations?

Answer: Agatha Brown, Jazzercise customer since 2012

"It took months for me to get 'talked into' trying Jazzercise. A few gals from my book club raved how awesome and fun it was, but I dismissed them, saying I was the girl who fell off the step in any sort of aerobics class. Then, a mom at my children's school worked on me, passing on every offer to bring a friend for a free weekend of Jazzercise, trying to get me there. Finally, I committed to a one-month-free pass.

"At the end of that first class, a handful of local moms from my kids' school came up to welcome me. Soon, one class turned into two, and I started practicing *chassés* and *triplets* at home. Songs and routines stuck in my head. Before I knew it, I was *in*—hook, line, and sinker—and I'm still in, six years later.

"I'm thankful that I finally got myself through the door and discovered what is now a special place in my life. It wasn't at all what I thought; it's so much more—not just a workout, it's entertainment, it's community, and it's fun!"

Question 2: What aspects of Jazzercise are most valuable to you?

What I'm really asking: As a representative of a key demographic, please pinpoint and prioritize your needs for me. Your answer can provide good intel on how to present the program to others in your socioeconomic and age sector.

Answer: Diana Mascarenaz, Jazzercise customer since 2003

"After a long day working at my corporate job, managing 17 employees and taking care of many, often challenging customers, I really look forward to my end-of-the-day Jazzercise class. I walk out the door of my office, often lumbering under the day's stress, and mentally prepare myself for class.

"What a pleasure it is to walk into the Jazzercise Center and have my instructor greet me by name, my fellow Jazzercisers happy to see me and eager to get started! I find myself surrendering to their positivity and to the physical challenges that every class represents. As a manager myself, I have great respect for the instructors who show up each day to motivate us to work hard and push us to achieve our fitness goals. At the end of each class, I feel remarkably stress-free, having left whatever HR issues or customer concerns behind me on the dance floor.

"I'm happy to have found Jazzercise and to have it be such an important part of my life. Two words surface when I think of it—fitness and camaraderie—and both, over the past 15 years, have significantly enriched my life."

Question 3: What would you say to a friend who is evaluating her fitness options?

What I'm really asking: Word-of-mouth is the best and cheapest form of advertising. How do our existing customers see and pitch the program to their friends? In our experience, many who use social media to badmouth a product or program are often chronic complainers. Happy customers tend to goodmouth us to friends and family instead of Yelp. They don't always bother telling us, because they think we know. What benefits are they highlighting? What language are they using?

Answer: Mindy Batt, Jazzercise customer since 1995

"I was in high school when a good friend invited me to join her at Jazzercise. After just a few classes, I was hooked! When I went away to college, however, there were no Jazzercise classes in my area, so I had to go to the local gym. Their classes were decent but nowhere near as fun or as challenging as the

Jazzercise classes back home. Four years later, after graduating, I picked up Jazzercise at the same center where I began and haven't left since.

"I can honestly say, and often have, that the best part of Jazzercise is that I've never been bored in class. In fact, it is more challenging now than it has ever been. I wake up excited, knowing that I will be able to go to class and have a blast dancing with friends. The instructors are inspiring, and the current mix of dance choreography and strength training is perfect—just what I need to stay motivated to show up five to six mornings a week. No matter what my day is like, it is always better after Jazzercise class."

Question 4: If you could change something about Jazzercise, what would it be?
What I'm really asking: I want to ask about negatives in a positive way. What are your pain points, that is, the needs or wants you've identified that we aren't fulfilling? Have they changed over time? What do we need to do better to give you what you need or want?

Answer: Lucille Henry, Jazzercise customer since 1978
"I started the program when I was 25 and never stopped. I've Jazzercised through three pregnancies, the loss of both my parents, and, five years ago, a hip replacement. The program, the instructors, and my great friends at Jazzercise got me *through*.

"Even though I'm in my sixties, I can still ride my 800-pound Harley motorcycle. It takes a tight core and real strength to hold it up and move it around. But I worry about muscle and bone loss. I'd like to have more strength training, not just to maintain but to improve, to push past the plateau and feel better and stronger today than I did yesterday. I also feel I need to work on flexibility—what I call functional fitness—so I can bend over, squat, sit on the floor, and get up without thinking about it."

Author's note: As a result of this input from Lucille and others in her age group, we recently expanded class offerings at her center to include half-hour strength classes and more stretch choreography.

Question 5: Is there anything else you'd like to share with us?

What I'm really asking: To me, this is the most open-ended of all the questions above. When you ask it, you must be prepared for anything. Usually, you'll get an earful. Good or bad, take the risk and listen with an open mind and, in Rosa's case, a grateful heart.

Answer: Rosa Rodriguez, Jazzercise customer since 1975

"I tell you, the best thing I ever did was join Jazzercise when I was 33 years old and, 44 years later, I'm still here. That's got to tell you something—and that something is Jazzercise!

"When I'm in class, I forget that I am 77 years old. I dance, smile, laugh, and breathe all at the same time. It is a wonderful feeling to do all that and to enjoy myself with 50 people or more, all doing Jazzercise.

"After class we often go for coffee and meet more Jazzercise friends. We talk about the new routines, the new moves, songs, and challenges that go with it. We also discuss our latest trips, parties, fashion, our children and grandchildren. Quite a few of us met over 40 years ago and have traveled to Jazzercise functions in Chicago, New Orleans, London, and Japan. We've made more Jazzercise friends there, from all over the world. I tell everyone: you should get in on this, too!"

CHAPTER 10

CLEF NOTES

♪ When you're in start-up mode with a small team, assessments and corrections happen organically. As you grow, however, a more structured assessment program is an important tool to make sure your key expectations are being fulfilled in the field. Handled properly, with respect, mutual understanding, and support, regular assessments yield multiple benefits to everyone involved.

♪ The key steps to any "inspect what you expect" efforts are clearly defining your expectations in the first place; leading with self-assessment and the opportunity for team members to self-correct or solicit help with any issues; completing a formal assessment to identify areas of strength and weakness; following up with positive, one-on-one coaching to support and reinforce progress and success; reassessing; then regularly repeating the whole process.

♪ Additional, often untapped sources for inspiring and improving individual and team performance are the superstars already on your staff. Invite them to create and record a presentation in which they share the secrets to their success, demonstrate effective techniques, and serve as an example to their far-flung peers.

♪ Regularly assessing your customers' satisfaction levels is equally important. In addition to traditional quantitative surveys, treat yourself to a more qualitative experience by personally connecting with your customers. Develop a handful of open-ended questions to ask one-on-one and listen carefully. Their answers may provide surprising insights you might otherwise have missed.

CHAPTER 11

The Joy of Giving Back

Caring people and companies care about giving back
through philanthropy, mentoring, and volunteering.
Giving back is the best reflection of who you really are.

Judi

There are many practical reasons to give back to the communities that support your business. Consultants will tell you that meaningful community outreach improves your corporate image and brand reputation. Business studies suggest it strengthens customer retention and stakeholder value. Rutgers University reports that employees who participated in employer-encouraged community or social outreach were 2:1 more satisfied with their jobs. As compelling as these facts may be, my reasons are more basic. When I was a girl helping my mother fill holiday baskets with food and gifts for needy families in our area, I learned that helping others was my social responsibility and personal privilege. As an adult, I've also learned that heartfelt giving back is as meaningful and enriching to the giver as to the recipient.

REACH OUT, RAISE FUNDS, GIVE BACK

You've heard the old saying, "Charity begins at home." I'd add, "In your business, charity begins at the top." If, as your company's top executive, you are committed to community outreach, you must encourage and empower your people to participate. In addition, while it may be tempting to dictate a companywide project, in my experience it's more meaningful to let local team members decide where and how their efforts could be most beneficial to their community.

In the past 50 years, our Jazzercise team has cumulatively raised and donated

> *"We make a living by what we get, but we make a life by what we give."*
> ⁓Winston Churchill

more than $32 million to charities within our communities. I could provide hundreds of examples but have selected these few to illustrate how giving back has worked for us and how it might work for you.

LEVERAGING CELEBRITY AND MEDIA FOR GOOD

In 1984, one of our earliest instructors, dynamic Jeri Sipe of Cleveland, Ohio, combined the three principles of our caring culture—care for self, care for others, and care for the community—into one terrific event. It was such a success on so many levels that it became a model that others in Jazzercise have followed for decades.

As I mentioned in Chapter 5, Jeri's husband, Brian Sipe, was the quarterback of the NFL's Cleveland Browns. At training camp, he and some of his teammates connected with a young fan, Robyn Schafer, who had cerebral palsy. When Brian asked Jeri if there was something they might do to support Robyn and the United Cerebral Palsy (UCP) of Greater Cleveland, she and her fellow area instructors conceived Jazzercise with the Stars. "We invited the general public plus Jazzercise instructors and customers in Ohio to join Brian and his teammates, plus Judi, and a bunch of Cleveland TV and radio personalities to Jazzercise for a good cause," Jeri said. I remember that night clearly. An amazing 6,000 people jammed the big ballroom of the Stouffer Inn on the Square in downtown Cleveland. All proceeds from participant admissions and sponsor donations were earmarked for UCP of Cleveland. The smile on sweet Robyn's face when we presented UCP with a check for more than $40,000 in her honor lit up the room. The following year, they did it again, raising more than $50,000. "Unforgettable," Jeri recalls, "and worth every bit of our volunteer efforts."

As news of the Ohio events circulated throughout the Jazzercise network, many others were inspired to give back in their area.

MARATHON DANCING AND NETWORKING FOR RESEARCH

For eight years, 1993 through 2000, Jazzercise instructors in the Chicago metropolitan area organized fund-raising dance marathons to benefit the Comprehensive Breast Cancer Center at Chicago's Rush Presbyterian-St. Luke's Hospital. Spurred by area manager Dani Gilmore Gresham, instructor Stephanie Dionesotes, and local "Wonder Woman" Dar Fraser of the Schaumburg area, these dance marathons soon spread nationally and internationally among Jazzercise studios in 100 other cities. Cumulatively, they contributed more than $3 million to the Breast Cancer Center at Rush. "Dar Fraser was easily one of Illinois's most successful and popular instructors," Dani says. "She and her group always topped the fund-raising charts for the Rush events. Years later, when Dar herself was diagnosed with breast cancer, she chose to be treated in the same superb facility that Jazzercise had helped fund. Her devoted customers were beside her every step through chemo and radiation. Remarkably, they continued to provide the same embrace of care to Dar's family after she lost her battle in 2010."

HIP-HOPPING FOR HOPE

For the past seven years in Orlando, local Jazzercise Center owners Patti Marshall and Patty Salvatore have cochaired a popular annual event called Hip-Hop & Hope, which brings hundreds of women together to dance with hip-hop icon Tim Roberts and to Jazzercise with our own charismatic Kenny

Harvey. All admission fees and participant-generated donations go directly to Florida Hospital's Breast Cancer Care Fund. "We are women helping women," Patti explains. "To date, we've raised $123,000 to assist the hospital's efforts in the prevention, prediction, detection, and treatment of local breast cancer patients." So far, the hospital tells Patti, Hip-Hop & Hope has enabled more than 900 uninsured women to receive free mammograms and has provided treatment to 40 diagnosed with breast cancer. "As the fund's second-largest contributor," Patti adds, "the Hip-Hop & Hope benefit is making a difference *and* our participants are having a great time doing so."

CELEBRATING SURVIVORS IN SAN DIEGO

In San Diego, Jazzercise Premier Center owner Susan Shofner is a two-time breast cancer survivor who, along with fellow instructor Terry Deneen, created the Save the Tatas Dance-a-thon for breast cancer awareness and research. In 2010 Susan and fellow instructor Andrea Singer rebranded the annual event as Jazzercise Dance for Life. Each October, during Breast Cancer Awareness Month, local instructors unite and invite other instructors and customers from all over the United States, Canada, and Japan to gather on the flight deck of the USS *Midway*, the giant retired aircraft carrier docked in San Diego Harbor. In 2018, more than 1,200 pink-shirted Jazzercise customers and instructors showed up to dance, celebrate the many, many breast cancer survivors among us, and donate the proceeds to breast cancer research and services. Last year, the event's six-year cumulative total of donations topped half a million dollars. "It is a labor of dedication, action, determination, and love," Susan says, "with Jazzercise as the glue that brought and keeps us all together."

When you encourage and empower your people to give back, be prepared to be amazed by their energy, creativity, and *results*. Their efforts will make a meaningful difference to your community and, according to all the research, their engagement will boost their workplace pride, commitment, and productivity.

PICK A PASSION POINT AND LET IT FEED YOU, AND OTHERS

Although money is always appreciated, there are many other things you as a company can give to enrich your local communities, including time, special talents, products, and services.

IN LIEU OF CASH, GIVE TIME AND TALENT

Each May, during National Physical Fitness and Sports Month, thousands of Jazzercise instructors volunteer at their local schools to provide free Kids Get Fit dance parties on school grounds. These events combine the latest popular music with high-energy, easy-to-follow dance moves and interactive fitness games. Their

> *"I have found that among its other benefits, giving liberates the soul of the giver."*
>
> ⸺Maya Angelou

message to each participant (including the one in every three kids who is considered overweight or obese) is that exercise can and should be fun!

We established Kids Get Fit in 1991 as a free community outreach designed to help schools promote kids' fitness as a way of life. Its popularity among our instructors and local schools has kept it going in all 50 states every year since.

More recently, in response to a personal challenge from First Lady Michelle Obama to "promote better health and boost self-esteem among the nation's young women," we created Jazzercise GirlForce, a global initiative launched in 2017 providing young women between the ages of 16 and 21 with a year of free fitness classes, no strings attached. Again, the program was so popular, the youthful energy of the girls so infectious, that many of our instructors have elected to continue the original one-year program to this day.

SHARE SPECIAL SKILLS WITH WORTHY PARTNERS

Although we have no structured programming for it, hundreds of our instructors regularly volunteer at local assisted living or retirement homes to provide older residents with free "lighter side" Jazzercise classes, including chair exercises for those confined to wheelchairs or the use of walkers. Many other instructors partner with local charity walks or runs to lead participants in a 15-minute series of warmup stretches prior to commencing the walk or race. It's a small but meaningful contribution to make sure everyone gets off to a safe, injury-free, and pain-free start.

Considering the skill sets of our instructors, their caring

natures, and their well-honed abilities to lead and encourage group activities, volunteer projects like these make perfect sense for us.

Assessing the skill sets of your people, what community-enriching volunteer activities might make sense for them? Don't feel like it's your job to come up with all the answers. You need only challenge them to think of ways they might be of service, then encourage them to follow through.

PROVIDE SPACE FOR THE ARTS

There are many worthy causes that need support—the environment, nature, health, education, the arts—and a wide variety of ways to help them. At Jazzercise, the performing arts are in our DNA. So, when founders of the fledgling New Village Arts (NVA) Theatre Group approached us with their need for space to rehearse and perform, we offered them temporary access to the back studio in our corporate headquarters. After five years of award-winning professional performances on our site, NVA emerged as the most critically acclaimed theater company in North San Diego County. Now based in a city-supported theater space downtown, they recently celebrated their eighteenth season and exceeded their annual revenue goal of $1 million. NVA executive director Kristianne Kurner says, "In our first five years, Jazzercise not only provided shelter, they gave us invaluable guidance and direction, and helped establish our reputation with local audiences, the critics, and the city. We literally wouldn't be here without them."

Be creative with your support. For years, we've opened the walls of our headquarters, for example, to local artists in a revolving biannual juried show. While we enjoy their art, they receive a six-month lease fee, plus the opportunity to expose and sell their work to the constant stream of local customers, vendors, staff, and visitors passing through our offices on a regular basis.

What worthy causes align with your company's DNA? How can you provide support to committed individuals and/ or organizations in a way that feeds you, them, and others in your community? Think outside the box. Options are every-where.

MAKE A DIFFERENCE, LARGE AND SMALL

Sometimes, when you're in start-up or rapid-growth mode and giving your all to your company, it's difficult to think about giving back to your community. I understand but would urge you to try something, no matter how small. Even a few hours or a single day spent helping others can make a difference—to them as well as to you.

> "No act of kindness, no matter how small, is ever wasted."
> —Aesop

Most of our franchisees are busy women leading very busy lives, but their capacity to care and to inspire others to join them means they make time to make a difference.

CHRISTMAS MITTENS FOR MINDY'S KIDS

Mindy Brown Ruiz is a full-time orthodontic dental assistant who also teaches several Jazzercise classes a week and, each fall, gets her customers involved in an effort they call Mindy's Kids. Fifteen years back, Mindy started small, when she learned from friends delivering toys to children in a Mexican orphanage that, although the kids were happy with the toys, they were also shivering in the cold of the Mexican hills. "I couldn't get the image of those shivering kids out of my mind," Mindy says.

Over the next few weeks, Mindy crocheted warm woolen scarves for the kids. Then she went to the dollar store to buy matching gloves or mittens. When she shared what she was doing with some of her Jazzercise customers, they wanted to help, too. "Some people knit; some people crochet; some people give money to buy the matching gloves or mittens. The first weekend in December, we all get together in the lobby of the Jazzercise Center and package one scarf or hat and a pair of mittens or gloves in a clear, one-gallon plastic bag. We always place the gloves or mittens on top so the kids can see before they open the bag that their hands will fit." The first year, Mindy provided 10 packages to the orphanage. Most recently, Mindy and friends provided more than 300 packages and helped deliver them to the orphanage, a local migrant camp, and the women's resource center. "It's a small thing but, when you're cold and shivering, we know it makes a big difference."

SHELTER MEALS ONCE A MONTH

Each Christmas for several years, Lynn Maas, our franchisee in Grass Valley, California, and her customers collected and donated funds to a local charity. Two years ago, they chose Hospitality House, a shelter that provides nourishing meals, medical services, a housing program, life skills, and job-training classes to homeless residents attempting to get back on their feet. The group set their goal at $395, the amount required to cover the shelter's food and other expenses for one night. They wound up raising enough money to support four nights.

Something happened, however, when they delivered the check. A group of nine Jazzercise women decided they wanted to take things one step further and commit to cooking one meal a month for between 55 and 75 Hospitality House guests. Tommie Conlen, who heads the Jazzercise team, explains, "It's so gratifying to prepare and serve a meal for guests who are so appreciative." To keep costs down, the team takes advantage of donations provided by the local Food Bank, grocery stores, and generous Jazzercise members. To keep things cooking, franchisee Lynn Maas offers first-Saturday-of-the-month classes in exchange for a donation in any amount to the Hospitality House Dinner Fund.

BOXES OF SOCKS FOR THE TROOPS

Many Jazzercise studios collect toys, fill baskets with food and gift cards, or raise funds for local charities over the holidays. In Albuquerque, New Mexico, Jazzercise instructors and customers regularly fill boxes of socks, hand and feet warmers, and packaged food for local Blue Star Mothers to send to those serving in the armed forces.

TRANSPORT TO DIALYSIS TREATMENTS

In Kuala Lumpur, Malaysia, Christina Yap rallied Jazzercise instructors, customers, family, and friends across the country to come together in a huge group dance event called Sweat2Smiles. Collectively, they raised enough money to provide the local MAA Medicare Charity Foundation with a new 12-seat mobility van needed to transport kidney patients to MAA centers for life-saving dialysis treatments, two dialysis machines, and a stress-test machine.

We are so proud of each of these efforts, large and small, as well as the hundreds of others our franchisees share with us each year. Certainly, they build goodwill for Jazzercise, Inc. More important, they confirm the goodness of caring human beings offering a hand to others who need it.

TAKE CARE OF EACH OTHER

It's no longer appropriate, the experts say, to describe the people who work with or for you as family. "You can't fire family," they say, adding, "calling coworkers family creates unrealistic expectations." Maybe so. But I have seen so many instances of the members of our far-flung company coming together with care and compassion that I'm at a loss as to how else to describe it. Let's just say that when you create a community of care, members of that community tend to care for each other. If that's not family, what is?

> *"Too often we underestimate the power of touch, a smile, a kind word, a listening ear, an honest compliment, or the smallest act of caring, all of which have the potential to turn a life around."*
>
> ⸺Author Leo Buscaglia

HOLIDAY HELP AND HUGS FOR HOLLY

When instructor Holly Galloway tragically lost her husband, Dave, in the December 9, 1999, crash of his US Marine CH-46 Sea Knight helicopter, her fellow instructors and customers rallied to make sure her three small sons, aged five, four, and one and a half, had a Christmas to remember. "Between the devastating news, the funeral, all the out-of-town visitors, I had very little energy or interest in Christmas that year," Holly recalls. "Then the doorbell rang, and there was Judi and others from Jazzercise with 10 boxes of toys and gifts for the boys, each one wrapped, personally labeled, and age appropriate. Over those holidays, and in the years that followed, Jazzercise wrapped its arms around us and I knew I was going to be okay." Holly is now a part of our corporate training team for new instructors. "It's kind of amazing that even today, 20 years later, my Jazzercise friends remember that the holidays can be a bit tough for me and they call, text, email me, send cards, or drop by my office for a hug at this time of year," Holly says. "I can't imagine what I would have done without them."

JOY AND LOVE FOR KEINA

In 2015, after months of painful stomach cramps, seven-year-old Keina Sakai, a Junior Jazzerciser in Hiroshima, Japan, was diagnosed with malignant lymphoma. "Throughout the whole experience—two abdominal surgeries and a series of chemotherapy," Keina's mom, Maya, says, "Keina's instructors and Junior Jazzercise friends visited her bedside. Keina was willing to fight so hard because she wanted to get back to her family and her beloved Junior Jazzercise so much."

Recently, Eri Sugano, associate instructor for Emi Sugihara, reported, "Keina won the battle! She's regained her strength and happiness and rejoined her friends, younger brothers, younger sister, and big sister at Junior Jazzercise class today!"

"There were smiles and love all around," added Maya, who takes adult classes. "To our family, Jazzercise is not just a fitness program. It's joy and love."

CARE AND REAL RELIEF IN THE WAKE OF NATURAL DISASTER

When Bastrop, Texas, instructor Stephanie Gordon lost her home to the most destructive wildfire in state history, Texas Jazzercise instructors and customers rallied around her with encouragement, cash, gift cards, and follow-up phone calls providing help. Similarly, when Northern California's disastrous 2018 Carr Fire destroyed the home of instructor Molly Redmon, Jazzercise studios all over the country responded with care and gift certificate packages for Molly *and* her customers affected by the fire. Also, in the wake of Hurricane Harvey's catastrophic flooding of Houston and southeast Texas, local Mary Wadsworth (our US Center sales director) reported, "The outpouring of love and care from Jazzercise franchisees worldwide was unbelievable. We received scores of gift cards directing us to help whoever needed it—instructors and/or customers."

I believe that how a person or a company steps up, gives back, and helps out is the best reflection of who they really are.

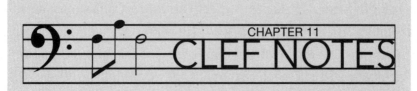

CHAPTER 11
CLEF NOTES

♪ As your company's leader, you have many responsibilities. It may be easiest to focus on financial responsibilities, as these appear most critical to your short-term goals. To survive long term, however, you must also focus on your social responsibilities. To thrive, you need to take care of those who helped you get there, both employees and customers, as well as the community that supported you. Looking at the big picture, it is a wonderful circle; if they are thriving, you will, too.

♪ Prioritize your support and charity by proximity. You'll not only help more deeply; your impact will ripple more widely. Take time to hear, see, and feel what's going on around you; think through the ways you can help; and empower others to take part. Look beyond your employees to your customers, your community, and finally your industry.

♪ Encourage your team to connect to a purpose greater than their day-to-day work. Leading a purpose-filled life can unleash potential in your team that you—and they—didn't even know existed. The effort and results can genuinely make a difference and send morale soaring.

♪ Giving back is not always about money. You can also provide talent, time, unique skills, and even safe, nurturing space to worthy individuals and organizations in your community.

♪ Often, small efforts can make as meaningful a difference as large ones. Don't feel you must "go big." Start small, observe and relish the results, then grow from there.

♪ Make an effort to take care of others, but also encourage others to take care of your own. Tragedies, personal crises, and natural disasters happen on an indiscriminate basis. When it happens to one of your own, encourage teammates to help any way they wish or can.

CHAPTER 12

Secrets to Our Longevity

Use your culture of care to create and maintain a solid community that will outlast the competition through continuous innovation.

Judi

In an economy where the average life cycle of S&P 500 companies has shrunk from 60 years to 20, in an industry characterized by short-term fads and transitory trends, how has Jazzercise survived for five decades? What lessons can we offer you to extend the life of your business as well?

This chapter is a compendium of ideas and information on the *whys* and *hows* of our experiences creating and re-creating—we live in a constant cycle of innovation—a long-term company in an often short-sighted economic environment.

WHY WE WORK IN 10-WEEK INCREMENTS

How frequently does your company create or revamp your product lines? How long does it take, from idea to implementation? How well does your new product cycle match your employees' and customers' needs, interests, and attention spans? The answers to these questions should drive your innovation efforts on a regular basis.

> *"To exist is to change, to change is to mature, to mature is to go on creating oneself endlessly."*
>
> —Philosopher Henri Bergson

At Jazzercise, we *know* that the enemy of fitness is boredom. For this reason, we completely update and revamp our core product—original choreographed dance routines to popular new music—every 10 weeks. (Early on, we had an 8-week iteration cycle but, through trial and error, 10 weeks proved to be our most realistic and comfortable turnaround time.) Why do we update so often? Because human nature and many studies dictate that performing the same repetitious exercises week in and week out increases a person's likelihood of giving up. Conversely, a constantly varied workout significantly improves motivation to continue. Supplying our instructors with 30-plus new, original routines every 10 weeks enables them to update and refresh their classes on a weekly basis. They know, as we do, that it's our unique blend of fresh new music and movement that keeps our customers coming back month after month, year after year.

Quite simply, our customers are the *why* behind our non-stop product reinvention five times each year. *How* we pull this off is a bit more complicated.

Each 10-week new-product cycle begins week 1 with a list of 60 to 70 potential songs that meet our stringent standards for use in a Jazzercise class—various musical genres; changing, energetic beats that pair well with our cardio and strength-training routines; fresh, positive lyrics; and creative, often unique sounds that inspire movement. My administrative assistant, Ginger Harris, pulls initial list options from several sources—*Variety*, *Billboard*, assorted music labels and companies, in-house recommendations, and online Studio suggestions from the field. The list contains a broad range of musical and dance genres, including jazz, hip-hop, funk, EDM/modern, pop/contemporary, lyrical, classical, Afro-Cuban, and Latin. Independently and together, Shanna and I cull our options to approximately 30 new songs, then decide who will choreograph which song to which class set objective.

Weeks 2 through 6, Shanna and I are actively choreographing in anticipation of week 7 pretaping of all routines. Our taping teams are a pool of talented Jazzercise instructors able to master new routines quickly, perform them properly, and adjust movements based on class formats. At pretaping, the list is finalized. That's when Young McCarthy and her training and development team begin their part of the process: compiling the written choreography notes that supplement each recorded routine and coordinating with our exercise physiologist for notes on specific muscle use, safety reminders, and teaching tips.

During weeks 8 and 9, our final-taping teams practice and master the new routines to perfection. In week 10, after two days of final rehearsals, taping commences in a professional studio, with three cameras and our excellent JM DigitalWorks production staff. Thanks to everyone's rigorous preparation, most routines are recorded in a single take.

Once taping is done, JM Digital's Dave Graack and Rich Sinatra edit the final Choreography Collection for worldwide distribution to our franchisees. As I mentioned in Chapter 8, on shipping days, our entire corporate staff used to gather to stuff envelopes and send 8,500 dupes of our newest collection on their way. Today, we post and stream new collections on our proprietary learning platform. The following week, we begin again.

On the surface, it may sound like the movie *Groundhog Day*—here we go again!—but there is a cadence and a rhythm to working this way. Like the baseline beat in music, our 10-week iteration drives other areas of the company as well.

In operations, for example, COO/CFO Sally Baldridge and VP of Operations Brad Jones, working with the technology team, apply cutting-edge Agile software development and Scrum methodology to develop our company and franchisee software. Scrum, a term borrowed from rugby, reconceives development as a team sport with frequent huddles, short-spurt iterations called sprints, and agile course tracking and corrections to get the job done in record time. Our marketing department, led by Allison Stabile, schedules and scales their promotions to coincide with the drop of each of our Choreography Collections. Similarly, Jazzercise Apparel designer and director Joan Marie Wallace and her team quick-step at double time to deliver *10* seasonal Look Books and studio-to-street apparel collections each year, online at www.shop.jazzercise.com for customers around the world.

Further, our sales managers, franchisees, and instructors eagerly track the Choreography Collections' process online to build customer buzz for the arrival of new music and routines. And our customers reward us with their regular attendance because, they tell us, "Jazzercise is never boring" and "there's always something new."

They need constant change to stay motivated, and we deliver it every 10 weeks. Do you know what your customers and employees need to stay motivated and active? How often do they need it? Are you delivering it at that rate?

HOW WE'VE REINVENTED OURSELVES EVERY 10 YEARS

In music, there are signatures and notations cuing a required change in time, tone, or intensity. In business, there are signs as well, signifying that it's time for you to direct a change or, just as often, that operational, market, or technological changes are directing you. Regardless of the source, it is critically important to stay

> *"Every act of creation is first an act of destruction."*
> —Pablo Picasso

nimble and receptive to the signs indicating the need to innovate and evolve in order to stay current, relevant, and alive.

TECHNOLOGY-DRIVEN CHANGE

In the 1970s, I started the business by teaching new choreography to other instructors at live Saturday afternoon sessions on the grass in my backyard. We could never have experienced the explosive growth of that decade without embracing its new technologies—video cameras and home DVR systems for training. The decades that followed encompassed the evolution from records to cassette tapes to CDs and, finally, today's instant downloading for music, with our training moved online. If you fail to respond effectively to the swift changes in technology, your business may fail as well. Thankfully, we've made staying up to date with technological advances a priority from the beginning. In the '70s, technology helped transform us from popular local classes to an international dance fitness phenomenon.

GOVERNMENT-DRIVEN CHANGE

In the '80s, government and IRS regulations forced us to completely restructure our business, from a relatively loose web of independent contractors to a highly regulated franchisor with thousands of national and international franchisees. This was a potentially disastrous, though ultimately successful turning point for us. I was blessed with excellent advisors who helped us navigate the regulators and the huge internal structural changes required. In addition, a strong management team and solid relationships with our instructors enabled us to effect their transformation from independent contractors to franchisees without losing anyone. Not one.

Surround yourself with good, strong, smart people (ideally smarter than you) who share your passion and support your purpose. Use complete transparency to build the trust that will help your team navigate unexpected changes, big and small, together. We started the '80s as a popular fitness firm and ended them as the second-fastest-growing franchise company in the United States. This leap would never have happened without trusted advisors and loyal, committed team members.

MARKET- AND SCIENCE-DRIVEN CHANGE

In our third decade, the '90s, the fitness industry, which had been in its infancy when we started, was now in full-blown young adulthood. Fit was it! And the options available in gyms, studios, public parks, and infomercials were mindboggling— from spinning to step aerobics, yoga to in-line skating, Tae Bo to Bowflex, ab rollers to ThighMasters. Despite such a crowded marketplace, we had great growth. However, when you've been around for 20 to 25 years, you start to experience natural transitions. Many of our best franchisees were "aging out," complaining that filling classes "wasn't as easy as it used to be," and considering retirement. These pressures, from both outside and in, necessitated a new business model.

To help drive more students to our instructors, we entered cross-promotional marketing arrangements with Nike shoes, General Mills' Total cereal, Ore-Ida potatoes, Mead

Johnson's Boost energy drinks, and Quaker Oats. Also, to stimulate enthusiasm among our franchisees, we devised a new incentive-based fee rebate program—a bonus for instructors who increased customers and revenues. This very popular President's Club motivated many of our more mature franchisees to refocus on their business, expand class offerings, and recruit new, younger instructors. Finally, in the face of all those 1990s fads, we concentrated on the science of fitness, participated in studies, and added a number of new class formats incorporating research-based step and strength training.

INTERNALLY- AND INTERNATIONALLY-DRIVEN CHANGE

The 2000s were our fourth decade and no less challenging than the decades before. I think of it as our "coming together" decade. Competition was fierce but, system wide, our sales were better than ever—record-breaking, in fact—year after year. Our focus was internal: keeping our franchisees and customers happy. We moved into new, custom-built headquarters, which brought all our divisions (franchising, JM DigitalWorks, and Jazzercise Apparel) together under one roof.

Our senior staff; my daughter, Shanna, who'd joined our executive team by then; and I logged millions of miles hosting very popular Jazzercise conventions in most major markets. We wanted to connect with our base, and to do so, we hosted 21 conventions in 2001 in England, Scotland, Italy, Mexico, and Japan, followed by 22 more in 2002. In 2003, they came to us by the thousands in Las Vegas. We were back on the road in 2004 through 2008, listening, engaging, strengthening ties with the Jazzercise faithful, and succeeding beyond all projections. In 2009, we gathered in Chicago to celebrate our fortieth anniversary and best year ever. The irony, however, is this: while we were busy nearly doubling our size domestically and internationally, the general public lost sight of us. The popular opinion was we'd somehow fizzled out like all those other '80s and '90s fitness fads. But we hadn't. Like many long-lasting brands, we did have a major PR and re-branding challenge ahead.

CUSTOMER-DRIVEN CHANGE

In the early 2010s, like most Americans, our franchisees and customers experienced the emotional and financial stresses of the Great Recession. Many, many of them told us that Jazzercise was one of the ways they got through it. We were there for them, and they were there for us. As things improved, our fifth decade involved yet another reboot. We rebranded—new logo, new signage, new studio standards, new class formats based on the new science of high-intensity interval training (HIIT). In addition to our regular class offerings at community-based parks and rec facilities, churches, and schools (which we now call satellite/community locations), many of our top franchisees opened dedicated Jazzercise Centers/Studios offering customers easier access to more classes, at a greater variety of convenient times. As the original boutique fitness company, our Jazzercise Centers represent an updated return to our roots and have quickly become a key new growth area for us. In addition, we anticipate further growth from our plans to provide Jazzercise video on demand (VOD), new methods to attract and maintain associate instructors, and a future off-shoot program targeting new audiences. We've also embarked on a decade-long campaign to raise our public profile once again, through a new website, an updated web-based learning management system for franchisees, a more assertive social media presence, and advanced PR. One of my favorite results was Shanna's high-profile feature in *Shape* magazine headlined "Jazzercise Is Back—and It Might Just Kick Your Ass!" We consider ourselves a force for fitness and we are focused on remaining vital.

In the summer of 2019, we will pause briefly to celebrate our fiftieth anniversary. But after the party—and it will be a big one!—we'll get back to the business of helping our customers achieve happier, healthier lives and to focusing on whatever challenges require change, inside or out, in our sixth decade.

Change isn't easy. Sometimes you must disrupt current mindsets to blaze ahead. For us, it's happened every ten years; in the future, it might be every five. Do what you must do. If you embrace the next new thing with honest excitement, genuine care, and complete transparency, your team and customers will be much more inclined and inspired to follow your lead.

THE GOOD, THE BAD, AND THE UGLY OF LEADING THE PACK

When you're the first at something, your focus is always forward, never backward. In the beginning, I was just doing what I loved, and I was thrilled that others loved it, too—enough to help me, join me, and take pride in this special thing we were creating and building together. The early days of any new venture can be intoxicating for everyone involved. And for those not involved, nobody really knows or cares what you're up to out on the new frontiers of your own invention.

I never planned to be a revolutionary in the world of women's fitness. Back in 1969, I just wanted women to show up for my class, have fun dancing to the beat of great music, and, over time, enjoy the ways rigorous exercise shaped them up, slimmed them down, and made them feel better about themselves. As you can imagine, there's great joy and satisfaction in trying something no one else has tried before and *succeeding* at it. I mean, that's the most seductive and rewarding thing about being an entrepreneur or revolutionary—following your own light instead of somebody else's—isn't it?

> *"Every revolutionary idea seems to evoke three stages of reaction: (1) It's completely impossible. (2) It's possible, but it's not worth doing. (3) I said it was a good idea all along."*
>
> —Writer Arthur C. Clarke

Being a revolutionary, however, can be a double-edged sword.

With success comes visibility, interest, imitation, competition, and unending demands to respond to or comply with new and constantly changing legal, financial, government, and market conditions. With early and big success, like we enjoyed, others begin adopting or adapting your innovations as "industry standards." On the downside, you become the target, the one to beat, the source of all kinds of misconceptions and, often, mockery.

When you discover that all your efforts have "suddenly" given birth to "an entire industry," you'll find it's much harder to stay on top than it was to get there. For us, the way through has been three-pronged: (1) we relentlessly focus on what's best for our customers, (2) we actively encourage, empower, and reward our team members for individual and group success, and (3) we stay open to change while never compromising our quality or integrity.

Over time, when you make mistakes, you must own them and, if possible, course correct. It's surprisingly easy, as we did, to become so mono-focused on building and bolstering your business and customer base internally that you forget to tell your story externally. While we quietly moved on to more and bigger success, a large part of our market assumed we were stuck in the '80s. We thought they knew better. They didn't because we forgot to tell them. We're working on that.

In addition, like chum in the water, the whiff of your industry-topping success will bring all manner of sharks to your door. You'll need a plan to deflect the near-constant solicitation from those eager to ride on your coattails, align with or co-opt your brand, gain access to your network, or potentially buy in, partner up, or take over your business. How you respond to potential buyers or investors will no doubt reflect the reason you got into your business in the first place. Personally, I reject the near-daily offers from venture capitalists and others to take Jazzercise "public." I've never been in it for the money—how much do you need, really? And I wouldn't be comfortable having unknown entities assume control of my team's livelihoods. When the offers come to you, my advice is to know yourself and you'll know what to do.

Finally, as a lifelong dancer, choreographer, entrepreneur, and CEO, I can't emphasize enough the importance of staying on your toes and maintaining flexibility. Stay sensitive to what's happening in your marketplace. Maintain awareness of your competitors, but don't chase them. (Most of them want what you, as pack leader, already have.) Keep busy doing what you do best and figure out ways to do it better. Most important, resolve to deliver to your customers whatever they need and want. And if at any time you don't know what that is, get out of your office and ask.

STAYING CURRENT AND VITAL, WHILE REMAINING TRUE TO YOUR CORE

Is it counterintuitive to think that your business can change constantly to stay current and vital to your customers while, at the same, your core values never change one iota? Not to me.

> "It's the job of any business owner to be clear about the company's nonnegotiable values."
>
> ⸺Restaurateur Danny Meyer

At the core of Jazzercise, and inside every one of our employees, franchisees, and instructors, is the ability to care—about each other, about our customers, and about the sense of community we form together. We hire caring people, we support them with in-depth training and high-quality products, and we recognize and reward their excellence, integrity, and caring behavior. In return, we are among those programs rewarded with the lowest turnover and the highest customer loyalty and repeat usage in the fitness industry. Further, two-thirds of our new customers are word-of-mouth referrals from existing customers. Although it may appear that we're in the dance fitness business, our true business is establishing and maintaining relationships and creating a caring community that helps everyone involved live healthier, happier lives.

We're not alone in thinking this way. Let me provide you with another example of remarkable longevity in a very different but historically trendy, often cutthroat industry.

Danny Meyer was 27 when he opened his first restaurant, Union Square Café, in New York City in 1985. Thirty-four years later, Meyer is CEO of the Union Square Hospitality Group, which includes more than a dozen high-end New York City restaurants and the global, billion-dollar chain Shake Shack. From the beginning, Meyer announced he wasn't in the restaurant business; he was in the hospitality business. To that end, he only hires people with a hospitable skill set:

genuine, happy, optimistic people who are naturally kind, caring, and empathic. "I can teach a nice person how to open a bottle of wine," Meyer says. "I can't teach a person who knows how to open a bottle of wine to be nice." He believes that employees who share their goodwill with customers create a positive relationship dynamic that drives the repeat business so critical to his restaurants' profitability. According to the Zagat Survey, Meyer's restaurants enjoy a record-breaking repeat business ratio of 70 percent. Regardless of his restaurant's concept, food, or location, "my goal," Meyer says, "is always to build a community of regulars."

Sound familiar? I thought so, too.

If you aspire to create longevity for your business, my recommendation is to get to know your core customers, build a culture of caring employees and policies around them, and never stop exploring new ways to serve them with quality programming, products, and services. Treat them like your life depends on them because, in every way, it does.

CLEF NOTES

CHAPTER 12

♪ Innovation fuels minds, companies, and industries. Being innovative stems from having an open mindset and paying attention to the cues signaling the need for change. What's your mindset? Are you open to new possibilities, excited by opportunities for growth, or fixed in the routine of your day-to-day "action items"?

♪ Schedule time each day to step back, set your ever-present to-do list or unexpected fires aside, and consider your core business and your customers' current responses. Are there signs your customers are getting bored or losing interest—more than a few squeaky wheels vying for your attention? Is there a pattern to their behavior that should be factored into your new-product development cycle? What's driving your cycle, your team's capabilities, or your customers' needs? Can you alter your processes to dovetail both in a timelier manner?

♪ In business and in life, change is constant and inevitable. The sooner you embrace this fact, the quicker you'll reap its benefits: life-changing personal and professional growth; flexibility forged by navigating tough challenges outside your control; insights derived from the balance of short- and long-term thinking; strength born out of continuous reinvention; and true camaraderie with those who share your mission and the journey.

♪ Although most things about your business will change over time, it's important to identify those things at the core—your values, your ethics, the quality of your commitment to your customers—that are the unchangeable essence of who you are and how your business will be. Clarify your core, communicate it to all involved, and in this one area, refuse to change or compromise. Whatever your longevity—5, 15, or even 50 years—you'll be glad and proud you did.

PART THREE

HARMONIZE YOUR BODY, MIND, AND SPIRIT

Happiness is not a matter of intensity
but of balance and order and rhythm and harmony.
—Thomas Merton

CHAPTER 13

Make the Body-Mind-Spirit Connection

Balancing your body, mind, and spirit helps you make the right decisions for the right reasons—not always for the bottom line, but for what is good and right and will be the best possible choice for everyone involved.

Judi

How many studies would it take to convince you that the science on the interconnectedness of your body, mind, and spirit is incontrovertible? The *American Journal of Preventive Medicine* published a review of 25 research studies over

> "If you don't live it,
> it won't come out
> of your horn."
>
> ⁓Jazz great Charlie Parker

26 years that confirmed "the impact of exercise goes far beyond the physical." Not being physically active can cause your body and mind to wither. Conversely, regular exercise causes a molecular chain reaction that improves mental cognition and processing, bolsters self-esteem and feelings of self-worth, and makes us significantly less prone to spirit-draining depression, anxiety, and malcontentedness.

As a leader, you owe it to yourself, your enterprise, and your team to make the connection that will enable you to function at peak performance levels in every aspect of your job and life. At the same time, you might encourage your employees to follow your lead. The same processes that benefit you will benefit your teammates and consequently your business as well. Simply put:

Care for your body = exercise.

Care for your mind = expand.

Care for your spirit = evolve.

Let's dive into these ideas further.

CARE FOR YOUR BODY

First things first: According to the Centers for Disease Control and Prevention, nearly 80 percent of adult Americans do not get the recommended amounts of exercise—two and a half hours of moderate-intensity or one and a quarter hours of vigorous-intensity aerobic activity each week. If you're one of them, it's time to get a move on. Why? Because, according to dozens of studies, physical inactivity can lead to obesity, excess belly fat, and increased risks for high blood pressure, type 2 diabetes, coronary heart disease, some cancers, as well as insomnia, fatigue, anxiety, and depression.

> *"Physical fitness is not only one of the most important keys to a healthy body, it is the basis of dynamic and creative intellectual activity."*
>
> ⁓President John F. Kennedy

Sobering stuff.

The good news is that no matter when or where you start, even a small increase in physical activity can have a big impact on your physical, mental, and spiritual health, as well as your overall sense of well-being.

> *"Dance first. Think later. It's the natural order."*
>
> ⁓Nobel Prize–winning playwright Samuel Beckett

In the past five decades of my involvement in the fitness field, I've seen firsthand the life-changing differences adding exercise can make in a person's life.

Regardless of your age, gender, weight, or physical ability, regular exercise will make you happier and healthier in at least eight ways that will impact the health of your business as well. Exercise does the following:

1. **Improves your brain function and memory.** Extensive research confirms that physical exercise alters the structure and function of your brain. Improved blood flow helps grow new blood cells and brain cells, which triggers new neurons and protects against brain cell degeneration. This translates into better focus and memory, quicker learning, less depression, and—as of now—the best way to delay or prevent the onset of Alzheimer's. Real-life benefit: the surprise expressed by younger team members over my ability to regularly create and teach dozens of newly choreographed dance routines without ever writing anything down.

2. **Shrinks fat cells.** Most people cite "losing weight" as their chief reason for exercising. And it is true that consistent aerobic exercise improves your body's ability to burn fat by providing enough oxygen to metabolize fat into energy. What's also true is that, in addition to weight loss, shrinking fat cells shrink their production and attraction of chronic low-grade inflammation, which is linked to a whole host of disorders, including (according to Vanderbilt University researchers) arthritis,

asthma, arteriosclerosis, high blood pressure, high cholesterol, cancer, and diabetes.

3. **Boosts your energy and combats aging.** Vigorous exercise is designed to get your heart rate up and your blood moving more rapidly throughout your body. Over time, improved cardiovascular health provides you with greater endurance and more energy to get things done. In addition, it slows the aging process at a cellular level. Real-life benefit: At age 55, my husband, Jack, ran his first triathlon. At age 65, he entered all six races in the San Diego Triathlon Series and finished first in his age group in all races, setting a new record for most points scored and outscoring all other triathletes, most of them much younger. Since age 70, Jack has competed in four national triathlon championships and qualified for four World Triathlon Championship races as a member of Team USA.

4. **Helps reduce pain, lighten mood, and relieve stress.** "For years, we focused almost exclusively on the physical benefits of exercise," says Cedric Bryant, chief science officer of the American Council on Exercise, "and really ignored the psychological and emotional benefits of being regularly active." Now, thanks to countless studies, the secret is out: exercise triggers the release of powerful brain chemicals—serotonin, norepinephrine, endorphins, and dopamine—that can help reduce

chronic pain, elevate your overall mood, relieve stress, and alleviate anxiety. Real-life benefit: My daughter Shanna explains, "To me, the true benefit of exercise is freedom. Freedom to do what you want—play with your kids, clean out your garage, do something you love—*without* pain, stress, or anxiety, and definitely *with* energy, comfort, and joy."

5. **Helps you sleep better.** Not just better, regular exercise also helps you sleep longer—up to one and a half hours longer—and deeper. This results in extended periods of slow-wave sleep, which is key to memory consolidation, physical recovery and repair, the recharging of energy stores, and the strengthening of your immune system. Real-life benefit: Researchers at Northwestern University divided a cohort of chronic insomniacs into two groups. One group remained sedentary and the other exercised regularly, getting two hours a week of moderate aerobic exercise. After 16 weeks, the active group reported improved sleep quality and duration, as well as improvements in their mood and quality of life.

6. **Is good for your muscles, joints, bones, and skin.** Although some may focus on certain exercises to build certain muscles, your entire muscular system benefits from the overall increase of blood and oxygen that regular exercise provides. Muscles require that blood and oxygen to remove cellular

waste and produce energy. And as your muscles push and tug and exert weight or pressure on your skeletal system, your bones are getting stronger, denser, and more stable, and your joints more lubricated with synovial fluid. Real-life benefit: Overhearing my teenaged granddaughter bragging to her friends that "my Jami can still do the splits . . . on both sides!" By the way, the same increased, oxygenated blood flow that benefits your muscles also nourishes your skin cells by delivering nutrients, removing toxins, and speeding up new growth.

7. **Enhances intimacy.** Beyond the obvious—that people who don't exercise often feel too tired or too out of shape to pursue sexual intimacy—there's the scientific evidence that the increased blood flow, energy level, and overall stamina generated by regular physical activity boosts sexual desire, arousal, and satisfaction among men and women.

8. **Is social and fun!** At Jazzercise, we've found that although most of our customers come to us for the reasons just cited—which are significant—they stick with us because they enjoy the sense of camaraderie and collective fun built into every class. They also contend that there's no chance of boredom because our instructors are always changing things up with new music, new routines, and new class formats on a regular basis.

There's wisdom in the adage that "the best exercise is one you'll *do*." If I've succeeded in persuading you to get moving, and I hope I have, I also hope you'll try a mix of low-, medium-, and high-intensity activities until you find the combination that invigorates your body, brain, and spirit. Aim for a minimum of two and a half hours a week of moderate aerobic exercise, or an hour and fifteen minutes a week of challenging, vigorous exercise. Don't forget to add in, as we do, some strength training a couple of times a week. As always, check with your doctor if you have any concerns or chronic problems.

EXPAND YOUR MIND

For many of the same reasons that it's important to exercise your body, it's equally critical to expand your mind. As your company's key decision-maker, you need to be able to think creatively to generate original thoughts, ideas, and business solutions. If your brain is stuck inside the box of ordinary, everyday problem solving, how can you break out? The same issues exist for your employees, too, so why not encourage their mind-expanding efforts as well?

> *"Feed your head."*
>
> —Grace Slick,
> Jefferson Airplane

Here are a few tips that work for me.

1. **Read and/or listen widely.** Broaden your perspective and potential by tapping into the cutting-edge

ideas of experts through their books, audiobooks, podcasts, and the often brilliant 18-minute TED talks at www.ted.com. Read books by leaders in your field and beyond. Search for new information and insight. Listen with curiosity and seek to understand others whose thoughts, opinions, or beliefs may run counter to yours. And there's nothing wrong with giving your brain a pleasure break by diving into a fast-paced mystery or thriller. You might pick up some intriguing insights into a new culture, time period, or travel destination.

2. **Join an organization or attend an event that stimulates your thinking.** Some years ago, I joined the Women Presidents' Organization, a nonprofit affiliation for successful women entrepreneurs (presidents, CEOs, managing directors) from diverse, noncompetitive industries. All are leaders of multimillion-dollar companies looking to take their businesses to the next level. The guest lecturers, roundtable discussions, collaborative peer projects, and the accomplished women themselves have been a terrific source of shared support, empowerment, inspiration, and wisdom for me. In addition, it was my attendance at the 2016 State of Women Summit that stimulated the idea for GirlForce, our global initiative launched in 2017 to support the growth and development of young women, aged 16 to 21. Put yourself out there; see what comes.

3. **Try something completely new.** Step outside your comfort zone to experience an afternoon, evening, or weekend from an entirely new perspective. Enjoy a night out at a theater, comedy club, or concert hall. Take a class, attend a lecture, visit a museum, or jump out of an airplane. Deliberately shift and shake up your day-to-day thought pattern. You may be surprised by what shakes out as a result.

4. **Seek out and study great minds.** Thomas Jefferson studied the work of English philosopher John Locke before writing the Declaration of Independence. John F. Kennedy studied Jefferson throughout his presidency. Martin Luther King Jr. was inspired by the peaceful teachings of Gandhi to lead the nonviolent civil rights movement. After Melinda Gates read the book *The Power of Half* by Kevin Salwen, about choosing philanthropy over consumption, she inspired her husband, Bill Gates; her billionaire friends Warren Buffett and Mark Zuckerberg; and others to pledge at least half of their wealth to philanthropic causes. When playwright Lin-Manuel Miranda discovered Ron Chernow's biography of Alexander Hamilton, the result was his Pulitzer Prize–winning rap musical *Hamilton*. Who in history inspires you? What can you learn, or be inspired to do, by studying them?

CONNECT TO YOUR SPIRIT

My first introduction to spirit was my mother telling me to "listen to your inner voice" and assuring me that "it will never steer you wrong." And, it never has. In fact, my only regrets are those times when I either didn't listen, or there were too many outside voices demanding attention that I didn't pause to hear what it was saying.

> *"Where the spirit does not work with the hand, there is no art."*
> —Leonardo da Vinci

Whatever you call it—your inner voice, intuition, emotional center, or higher self—your spirit enables you to make decisions and solve problems intuitively and effortlessly. All it asks is that you listen and connect on a regular basis. How? I can recommend the following from long, often hard experience.

1. **Make time to do nothing.** As CEO of a global enterprise, I am as overcommitted as you are. For a few minutes each day, usually early or late, I take time to sit by myself and simply breathe. I aim to be completely "in the moment," mindful of the sights and sounds of my surroundings yet focused on the feelings that surface when given the time and space to do so—joy, happiness, concern, pain, sadness, grief, whatever. I listen for whatever my inner voice has to say or, if she's quiet, I simply embrace the silence. This is

my version of meditation. I encourage you to find yours.

2. **Create spontaneity, expect serendipity.** My natural tendency is to be very organized and try to keep everything under control. I have learned, however, to make a conscious effort to let go of my need for control. (Surprisingly, things get done very well without me micromanaging them.) Through wonderful and challenging experiences, I've discovered that much of life isn't controllable, and the unexpected often yields life-changing opportunities. Also, it's a lot more fun to loosen up and be less "tight-assed." I make room for spontaneity—to act on a good intention, make the unexpected phone call, celebrate the completed project or accomplished goal, recognize a team member's significant work or wedding anniversary, and acknowledge the changing seasons and holidays in some new and novel way. Some of the best breaks I've had recently were last minute and completely unplanned. A one-day fly-in to Las Vegas with Jack to see our granddaughters perform in a national dance competition, a rambling road trip to Texas with no reservations, a weekend with my cousins at the Iowa State Fair—pure joy. When you crack open your personal door to the unexpected possibilities just outside your comfort zone, I guarantee the amount of light that comes flooding in spontaneously, serendipitously, will surprise and delight you.

3. **Take time to connect with loved ones.** That trip to the state fair with my Iowa cousins reinvigorated the connections we'd had as young kids. The road trip with Jack to Texas and back was refreshing and rejuvenating for both of us. Going for coffee after class with longtime customers has resulted in great and special friendships. A peaceful 20-minute walk with my dogs, a phone chat with my son, or a lunch and shopping date with my daughter and grand-daughters at the local mall puts gas in my tank like nothing else can. Never underestimate how much spending even a small amount of time with loved ones can elevate your sense of well-being and re-connect you to your and their spirit.

4. **Practice gratitude from A to Z.** Here's a challenge I give myself on a regular basis and I'm happy to share with you. On a blank piece of paper (or smartphone notepad, if you prefer), write the name of a person, situation, or experience you're grateful for that begins with the letter *A*. Now move on to *B*, *C*, and so on, all the way to *Z*. It's a simple exercise, but an important reminder that will lift your mood, improve your perspective, and reconnect you to the bigger, better spirit that lives inside all of us. One warning: it may also suggest people or tasks that require attention, acknowledgment, or amends. Accept that as your spirit talking to you, gently nudging you to be your best self and live your best life.

MAKE THE CONNECTION, MAKE A DIFFERENCE

> "I have one life and one chance to make it count for something. . . . My faith demands that I do whatever I can, wherever I am, whenever I can, for as long as I can with whatever I have to try to make a difference."
>
> ⸺President Jimmy Carter

The title of this book is *Building a Business with a Beat*. I urge you to never lose sight of the fact that in building your business, you're also building a life for yourself, your family, and the surrogate family members who choose to spend most of their days and much of their lives advancing your mission. Make it count, make it worthwhile, and as our Nobel Peace Prize–winning former president says, "Make a difference."

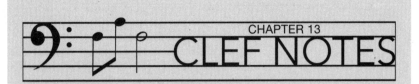

CHAPTER 13

CLEF NOTES

♪ What is your definition of success? It's easiest to say, "reach my business and financial goals." But will you also add "achieve physical, emotional, and spiritual well-being"? Researchers at Harvard Business School confirm that doing so *will* make you a better decision-maker and business leader, as well as a happier human being. Would you also consider adding "avoid burnout, dissatisfaction, and disconnection by exercising my body, expanding my mind, and connecting to my spirit on a regular basis"? I hope so! In this book, I've suggested a lot of things you could or should do. My final challenge to you is to start with one idea or suggestion that resonated with you. Which Clef Note gave you pause, set your synapses snapping, prompted your own inner voice to say, "Yeah, yeah, that's right!" Start there.

♪ Now, start small if you must, but change what you are doing and—here's the key—designate a trusted friend, family member, or an app (anything outside of yourself) to hold you accountable to making that change or achieving that goal. Have them meet you there, follow up with you, and serve as your own personal cheerleader or coach.

♪ I'm in fitness, the single most commonly made and broken New Year's resolution, and I can guarantee you that if you can keep a change going for 66 days (that's a scientific fact) you are more likely to keep it up for the rest of the year and beyond. Take the step, make the call, change the mindset, then keep going! How? See Chapter 14, "Keep Moving Forward."

♪ Need more help or motivation? Visit our website, www.Jazzercise.com, and find a class near you. Tell the instructor "Judi sent me" and let her know why you're there. The struggle can be real. We'll make whatever you're attempting easier, less stressful, and way more fun!

CHAPTER 14

Keep Moving Forward

Anyone who knows me well knows my mantra is "keep moving forward." I learned it from my mother, who no doubt picked it up from her Swedish immigrant father, who came to America as a teenage farmhand. By the time he died, he'd amassed five farms of his own, spanning hundreds of fertile acres, and served his southwest Iowa community

> *"And the beat goes on . . ."*
>
> ⸺Sonny and Cher

as a popular county commissioner. The Swedish version of "keep moving forward" is *titta inte tillbaka, du går inte så,* or "don't look back; you're not going that way."

Given my innate preference to always focus on what is in front of me, writing this book and looking back over a lifetime spent pursuing my passion and attracting others to our shared purpose has been a challenge for me.

WHAT I LEFT OUT

When I began this project, I made the conscious decision that this book would be as much about you—the start-up entrepreneur, the owner, founder, CEO of your company—as it was about me and Jazzercise. What I didn't expect from this book was how much I would learn about myself as I sifted through the files, notes, and memories of the past five decades.

> "In a good book the best is between the lines."
> —Swedish proverb

Rediscovering my mother's obituary from May 8, 1986—three days before Mother's Day that year—I was reminded how little time I allowed myself to truly grieve her loss. I've written about how pivotal she was to my development as a dancer, a businesswoman, and a woman, but I didn't share one of the biggest regrets of my life: that I wasn't there when she passed.

It was the mid-1980s, the company was growing at warp speed, and, although I flew in to see her in Iowa several times that spring, I missed our final good-bye. In addition, I remember brushing past the fact that she died of amyotrophic lateral sclerosis (ALS, Lou Gehrig's disease) and refusing, over Jack's objections, to get tested for any genetic or familial link.

Ten percent of ALS cases are considered familial, but whether hers was or not, I didn't want to know, and I simply moved on. It's the classic entrepreneur's dodge—*I can't deal with this now; I have a company to run, remember?*—which, over the long haul, I do not recommend.

While having both passion and purpose is critical to your company's success, finding the balance between your work and your life as a spouse, a child to your older parents, a parent to your children, and a friend to those you cherish is crucial to your personal happiness and success as a human being. I can't offer any easy answers or magic equations here; only the painful truth that, in the end, no one—no matter how successful they are—wishes they'd spent more time working and made less time for their loved ones.

One genetic link I *am* certain I shared with my mother is the Swedish propensity to keep private things private. Whatever marital ups and downs Jack and I experienced, whatever parenting or health challenges we've faced, I chose to leave "between the lines." Save one.

In October 2018, I did decide to make one very private experience public. I was attending our largest fund-raiser in support of breast cancer research and services, on the flight deck of the USS *Midway* in San Diego. Surrounded by more than 1,200 pink-shirted Jazzercise customers and instructors, many of them proud breast cancer survivors, I decided it was the right time and place to share that, four years earlier, I'd become a survivor myself. In 2014, I had skipped a mammogram, found a lump, learned it was malignant, had a lumpectomy, and completed radiation—all while continuing to work and telling no one except my husband, Jack; daughter, Shanna; son, Brendan; personal assistant, Ginger; and our COO, Sally Baldridge.

Not having to endure chemo and the loss of my hair made it easier to keep the whole thing a secret. In retrospect, my reasoning—this was a private matter—reflected both my own concerns as well as my unwillingness to cause concern among my far-flung team members. I was lucky to be able to work through treatment, to have Jack's, Shanna's, Brendan's, Ginger's, and Sally's unwavering support, and to arrive on the other side at NED—no evidence of disease. It was with great relief and gratitude that I finally decided to share my story, raise awareness of the ubiquity of breast cancer and the need for mammograms, and claim my place among the celebrating survivors. Should I have made the decision to share this part of my story earlier? It seems to me that each person must make the best decision they can at the time they make it. Good decision or not is immaterial because, either way, you learn from the past and keep moving forward.

Sadly, as this book was in final copyediting, Jack's and my life took another hard turn. Our 36-year-old son Brendan—a wonderful artist in the middle of assembling a prestigious one-man show—relapsed to his disease of addiction and passed away. Losing your child is every parent's worst nightmare. When addiction is the cause, the stigma, misunderstanding, and judgment surrounding the disease can add another level of pain to the loss for surviving family members and friends. In memory of our beautiful, intelligent, creative son and in hope that we can help other vulnerable artists and their families sidestep our disastrous outcome, we are creating the nonprofit The Brendan Project. For more information, please visit www.TheBrendanProject.org.

WHERE DO WE GO FROM HERE?

In June 2019 Jazzercise will celebrate the end of our fifth decade and the beginning of our sixth. There will be a brief, fun-filled pause, and then we'll begin again, as we have in every other decade, the never-ending process of reinvention. There will be the changes we ourselves initiate, such as company structure, new programming, and product development. And there will be the surprises we have no control over, in market forces, government regulations, technological advances, and, most important, our customers' needs.

In any entrepreneurial company of any age, it never ends. Would you really want it to? Unless your objective is to sell out and retire, you have no alternative but to continually analyze what you do best, figure a way to do it better, and keep your people moving forward.

How? In jazz music and dance, there's a key element called syncopation, which involves a strong, distinct rhythm that makes you want to move. The best DJs know all about this. When the dance floor is empty, and the walls are full of people looking around for something to do, a great DJ

> *"And now we welcome the new year, full of things that have never been."*
>
> —Poet Rainer Maria Rilke

knows it's time to upset the meter, shift the accent off-beat, and increase the group's desire to dance. You've been there, and I bet you've found yourself suddenly dancing to the syncopated delights of Bruno Mars's "Uptown Funk," Beyoncé's "Single Ladies," Luis Fonsi's "Despacito," or Justin Timberlake's "Can't Stop the Feeling." Right?

"But, Judi," I can hear you asking, "how does that translate into a business setting?"

Syncopation in business means orchestrating, welcoming, and incorporating the element of surprise to keep things interesting and moving. Anything out of the ordinary, anything that adds the unexpected to a predictable pattern, anything that moves the emphasis from the strong, straight ahead, 4/4 downbeat to a different off- or backbeat is syncopation. (Frank Sinatra was a master at it, as was Amadeus Mozart, Bill Gates, and Steve Jobs.) It's what drives a dancer's pivot, a pitcher's changeup, and a quarterback's sneak. In business, it means challenging your teams to redefine their perceived mission and boundaries, reenvision your customers' experience, rework your business model, and reimagine the use of your technology assets.

At Jazzercise, we thrive at a distinctly syncopated beat. What's the rhythm in your workplace? Where in your company can you feel the heat, the beat that sets toes tapping, fingers snapping, synapses zapping, and movement happening? Figure it out and spread it around. While you're at it, add some hip music to your company playlist. And, at your next big meeting, when the movement and the magic just isn't happening, do what DJs do: take a break, turn up a syncopated classic, stand up and stretch, and try not to dance. I promise you this small exercise will boost the beta waves in everyone's brain, improve the group's connection, and up the energy for a more creative outcome.

KEEP GOING . . .

In the previous chapter, I noted that one way to expand your mind is to choose and study the thoughts and ideas of an inspirational role model. Years ago, I chose Harriet Tubman, a runaway slave who, rather than simply relish her freedom, made 13 return trips into the South to personally escort more than 70 fugitives to freedom. "I was the conductor of the Underground Railroad for eight years," Harriet said, "and I can say what most conductors can't say—I never ran my train off the track, and I never lost a passenger."

> "If you are tired, keep going. If you are scared, keep going. If you are hungry, keep going. If you want to taste freedom, keep going."
>
> —Attributed to Harriet Tubman, conductor on the Underground Railroad

During the Civil War years, Harriet served the Union as a nurse and a spy, slipping behind enemy lines to gather information on troop placements and supply lines. After the war, she helped hundreds of newly emancipated slaves transition to the life of free men and women. She also joined forces with Elizabeth Cady Stanton and Susan B. Anthony in the fight for women's suffrage.

Although I can't begin to imagine the challenges and dangers Harriet Tubman faced while escorting slaves north to freedom—the distance between her times and life and ours is immeasurable—I can admire her commitment to helping others achieve a happier, healthier, more empowered life for themselves. Of all the things that Jazzercise has accomplished over the past 50 years, I am most proud of our role in assisting millions of men and women improve their quality of life and health through fitness and the joy of dance. Further, we've provided thousands of women with the opportunity to create their own businesses and to redefine themselves as strong, independent businesspeople and successful business owners.

To me, Harriet's long-ago message to the "passengers" she was conducting to safety and freedom still resonates: Keep going. If you're tired, keep going; if you're scared, keep going; if you're hungry, keep going; if you want to taste freedom, keep going.

In today's world, whatever experiences you've had in the past, whatever hopes, intentions, or plans you have for the future, I believe the secret to staying on track between those two points is to keep moving forward. Follow your passion, make helping as many people as possible your purpose, trust your inner voice, and, above all, keep going!

NOTE TO
MY GRANDDAUGHTERS

*(and anyone who aspires to make a life and living
doing what they love)*

Dear Skyla and Sienna,

When I watch you dance, my heart does flip-flops and pir-ouettes and *jetés*. You bring such joy to the art form, your audience, and me! You may not realize it now, but your passion for dancing, your determination to be the best you can be, *every* time you perform, is creating a deep well of strength and self-knowledge you'll be able to draw from for the rest of your life.

Having a God-given talent is never enough. But when you pair it with hard work, discipline, and a strong will, you will become capable of achieving anything you set in your sights. Be confident in who you are and the passion that colors everything you do.

Right now, your focus is on channeling that passion into performance. Do that! Master your art, perfect your craft, become the best you can be. Later, if you choose, you can redirect all the mastery, all the expertise you've picked up along the way, in service to a higher purpose, one that only you can devise and deliver to help others improve, expand, or better enjoy their lives. That power is within you; go there and listen to the strong, supportive inner voice that only you can hear. She will never steer you wrong.

It has been one of my life's greatest blessings to be a part of your lives since you were born, and to watch your mother raise you to embrace the values my mother and grandmothers held dear: integrity, humility, kindness, and compassion for others. They taught me, as your mother and I have attempted to teach you, how important it is to speak your truth and remain authentic. You are both becoming strong, principled young women. Never forget, or let anyone dissuade you, from the fact that you have a right to your voice, and you must defend that right whenever you feel it is necessary.

I hope you'll also remember to "use your gut, your head, and your heart"! Go with your gut feelings, use your head when making decisions, and tune into the love and the goodness in your heart.

I love you beyond whatever you can imagine, my sweet girls. And I can't wait to see and celebrate the bright, beautiful ways you'll find to make this world a better place.

Love,
Jamie

ACKNOWLEDGMENTS

Heartfelt thanks to each and all the folks mentioned here. Without your help, hard work, and creativity, the feats accomplished, lessons learned, and passionate lives and experiences we shared together at Jazzercise might have remained a batch of collective memories instead of the very real book you're holding in your hands.

Jill Marr	Ace literary agent at Sandra Dijkstra Literary Agency, Del Mar, California
Cheryl Segura	Fellow dancer and editor at McGraw-Hill Education, New York, whose keen insights helped make this a better book
Susan Carol McCarthy	Writer, good friend, and wizardess of words
Kenny Harvey	Jazzercise vice president and go-to guy whose level of dedication and hard work always, without fail, exceeds expectations
Megan Wakefield	Jazzercise HR director, clear, creative thinker, and a calming force
Ginger Harris	Personal assistant extraordinaire who keeps me sane

Celine Borie	Special assistant and invaluable utility player
Allison Stabile	Jazzercise marketing director who is always looking ahead and pushing forward
Katie McClain	Senior graphic designer and image maker
Julika Kade	Graphic designer for Jazzercise Apparel and whatever else we need
Jeff Lancaster	Cover photographer and visual memory keeper
Dylan, Pancho, and Frank	My four-legged furry friends who love me unconditionally and make sure I get walked
Brendan Missett	My wonderful, supportive son, for the always well-timed words of encouragement and big heart-to-heart hugs
Shanna Missett Nelson	Jazzercise president and my smart, beautiful daughter, for working so hard, being so creative, and having the patience to put up with me
Jack Missett	My husband, best friend, and exceptional pack rat who kept all the records intact, remembered where the memories were buried, and knew just how to dig them up

Finally, wholehearted thanks to every person who took the calls, answered the emails, searched your files, shared your memories, provided background information, or told the individual stories that appear in this book. Your kindness and generosity of spirit helped me fill in the blanks and complete the picture of our communal mission and the shared journey of Jazzercise over the past five decades. I could not have accomplished any of this without you.

INDEX

Acri, Claudia, 84
Acri, Kathleen, 84, 96
advertising, 110, 186
Aesop, 201
aging process, exercise and, 235
Albright, Madeleine, 122
Alzheimer's disease, 234
amyotrophic lateral sclerosis (ALS), 248–249
Angelou, Maya, 1, 198
Anthony, Susan B., 253
Apodaca, Jerry, 95, 96
Armstrong, Louis, 160–161
audiences:
    as business consideration, 79–80
    as creative consideration, 10, 17, 25
    as entrepreneurial consideration, 37–38
    teaching and, 29–34
    (*See also* customers)
Auker, Fran, 93

Baby Huey & the Babysitters, 20
Baldridge, Sally, 214, 250
Batt, Mindy, 169, 186–187
Beckett, Samuel, 233
Bergson, Henri, 212
Bezos, Jeff, 132
Bircher, Berra, 127–128
Blake, Janece, 96
Blue Star Mothers, 204
Brady, Nancy, 168
brain function, exercise and, 232, 234

branding, 66–67, 92, 108, 110, 129–130, 193, 219
Branson, Richard, 167
breast cancer, 196–198, 249–250
The Brendan Project, 251
Brodie, Karen, 62–63
Brown, Agatha, 184–185
Bryant, Cedric, 235
Buchanan, Peggy Marchbanks, 109
Buffett, Warren, 240
bureaucracies, 51–52, 124–125
Buscaglia, Leo, 205
Bush, George H. W., 136
business plan, 77–78, 102

cardiovascular health, 235
Carlsbad Parks and Recreation, 48–52
Carter, Jimmy, 244
Casper (Wyoming) *Star Tribune*, 43
Cates, John, 48
change:
    adapting to, 216–227
    sustaining, 246
charitable giving:
    approaches to, 208–209
    arts programs and, 200–201
    fund-raising events in, 94, 194–199
    by Jazzercise franchisees, 201–207
    motivations for, 193–194, 240
children:
    charitable events for, 202
    fitness programs for, 84, 136–138, 198–199

A Chorus Line (Broadway show), 48
Churchill, Winston, 194
Clarke, Arthur C., 221
Coats, Reverend Walter R., 123–124
Cole, Marsha, 62–63
companies:
    adapting to change, 216–227
    average life cycle of, 211
    communication within, 88–89
    disruptive, 106–108, 117
    esprit de corps in, 89–91, 103
    evolution of, 141
    values practiced by, 150–152,
        155–157
company culture, 141–157, 168, 175
competition, dealing with, 222–223
Comprehensive Breast Cancer Center
    at Rush Presbyterian-St.
    Luke's Hospital (Chicago), 196
Conlen, Tommie, 203
consultants, 70–72, 75
control, relinquishing, 60, 142–143,
    242
core business, identifying, 225, 227
Crystal Geyser, 132
customers:
    assessing satisfaction of,
      182–189, 191
    brand experience created for,
      160–173
    company culture and, 145, 225
    listening to, 116, 223
    motivating, 215
    primacy of, 105, 110, 117, 118
    reaching, 110–112, 180–182
    referrals by, 165, 166, 186, 224
    retaining, 105, 153, 161, 165,
      169, 193, 224, 225
    trust from, 170–171
    (*See also* audiences)
customer touchpoints, 161, 163,
    172, 184

dance:
    physical fitness and, 27–29, 143
    practice as important to, 152–153
    syncopation in, 251–252
    as universal language, 100
    (*See also* jazz dance)
dance marathons, 196–198
Dance Mixx, 116
Davidson, John, 87
Davis, Ian, 143
Davis, Miles, 55
delegating responsibility, 59–60, 74,
    84–85, 101, 103
Deneen, Terry, 197
"Dinah!" (TV show), 65–66, 86–87,
    131
Dionesotes, Stephanie, 196
Disney, Walt, 102
Donahue, Phil, 87
dreams, achieving, 112–114, 117
Dunkel, Priscilla, 100

Eckstine, Billy, 170
Elizabeth II (queen of England),
    147
Emerson, Ralph Waldo, 115
employees:
    charitable giving and, 193, 194,
      198, 200, 208–209
    customer care by, 225
    empowering, 143–144, 147
    encouraging fitness in, 232
    as family, 204–205
    hiring, 62, 85–89, 145–146,
      156
    independent contractors as, 68
    performance metrics for,
      175–182, 190–191
    sense of purpose of, 144–145,
      208
    termination of, 46–49, 53
    trust in, 101, 102, 142, 171

empowerment:
  of employees, 143–144, 147
  of women, 239
energy level, improving, 235
Entrepreneur magazine, 109
entrepreneurship:
  business growth and, 69–72, 77,
    78, 83–85, 103
  case studies on, 93–101
  cash flow and, 50
  change and, 226–227, 251–252
  charitable giving and, 194, 201,
    208–209
  company culture and, 157, 175,
    211
  delegating responsibility in,
    59–60, 74, 84–85, 101, 103
  economic conditions and, 79
  employee performance and,
    175–182
  finding employees and, 85–89
  franchising vs. independent
    contractors in, 68–69,
    216–217
  interpreting business signals in,
    58, 73, 74
  of Jazzercise franchisees, 122
  leadership and, 148–149, 152, 156
  merchandising in, 66
  motivation for, 141, 170, 221
  need for respite from, 241–243
  pitfalls of success in, 222–223
  sense of purpose in, 34–37
  technology use in, 64–65, 102
  trust as essential to, 170–171,
    173, 217
  use of consultants in, 70–72, 75
  wider impact of, 244
  women in, 239
  work/life balance and, 249
  zeitgeist and, 79–80, 102
Equal Opportunity Act, 50

Feherty, Bill, 98
Field, Ron, 111, 113
Florida Hospital Breast Cancer Care
    Fund, 197
Ford, Henry, 154
Forrester's Customer Experience
    Index (CX Index), 160, 172
franchises:
  celebrating milestones in, 167
  company growth and, 109
  incentive plan for, 133–134
  vs. independent contractors,
    68–69, 216–217
  management style and, 143–144
  royalties on, 69
Fraser, Dar, 196

Galloway, Dave, 205
Galloway, Holly, 205–206
Gambill, Joan Missett, 151, 153
Gaslight Club (Chicago), 17–18,
    22, 23
Gates, Bill, 35, 183, 240, 252
Gates, Melinda, 240
gender:
  fitness differences and, 27
  payscale and, 49–51
General Mills, 132, 217
Giordano, Gus, 13–18, 20–23, 29,
    31–32, 36, 39, 42–43, 113
Giordano, Peg, 21, 39, 42–43
Giordano Jazz Dance Chicago, 13,
    14, 80
Golden Door spa, 45–47
Gordon, Stephanie, 206–207
Graack, Dave, 214
Graham, Martha, 152
gratitude, as practice, 243
Great American Fitness Workout,
    136
Great Recession, 219
Green, Stan, 67–68

Gresham, Dani Gilmore, 121,
122–123, 196

Halley, Karen, 84
Hamilton, Shirley, 16
Hamilton (musical), 240
Happy Medium (Chicago club), 20
Harris, Ginger, 213, 250
Harvey, Kenny, 126–131, 135–136,
196–197
Henry, Lucille, 187–188
Hepburn, Katharine, 107
Hillerman, Anne, 96
Hip-Hop and Hope benefit, 196–197
Hospitality House (Grass Valley, CA),
203
hypermobility, 9

independent contractors, 68–69,
216–217
industrial theater shows, 16–17
inflammation, exercise and, 234–235
infomercials, 71, 72
Ingenious Designs, 36
innovation:
company longevity and, 211–212
customer-oriented, 105–106
cycles of, 212–215
recognizing need for, 215–216,
226
Internet, business start-ups
and, 80

James, Mary, 88
Janikas, Bobbi, 114
Japan, 128–129
jazz dance:
first studio for, 14
hybridized, 40–41
as narrative, 15
public interest in, 48
teaching of, 29–33

Jazz Dance for Fun and Fitness
(class), 32, 33, 35, 36, 40, 45
Jazzercise:
benefits of, 153
books published by, 86
business plan for, 78
certification program for, 109
charitable giving and, 194–207
children's programs in, 70–71, 84,
199, 239
choreography for, 61, 213–214
company culture at, 148–151,
168, 171, 194–195
core business of, 147, 224
corporate alliances with, 132,
217–218
customer experience of, 161–169,
170–171, 183–189, 215, 237
customer retention rate for,
105–106, 153, 161, 169, 224
Decade of Firsts for, 115
early influences on, 13, 15, 17, 23,
35, 107
factors in success of, 78–81,
91–92
financial recession and, 133–135,
219
finding class locations for,
121–124, 132
finding employees for, 85–89
franchise case studies, 93–101
franchise structure of, 68–69, 90,
92, 133–134, 216–217
growth of, 60, 62, 63, 67, 69–72,
81, 90–92, 100, 116, 132,
219–220
impact of, 254
innovations associated with,
107–108, 218
international conventions for, 218
learning management system for,
154–155, 180, 214, 220

Jazzercise (*Cont.*):
longevity of, 143, 211, 218–220, 251
management style at, 142–144
meetings held by, 89–90, 149, 154–155
merchandising by, 66, 71–72, 129, 135
music acquisition for, 87–88, 213
naming of, 33
ownership of, 59, 61, 223
philosophy behind, 107, 222
product update cycles in, 212–215
programs in, 116
promotions for, 86–87, 110–112, 135–136, 152, 181, 217–218
reinvention of, 219–220, 222, 251
rewards programs and, 166–167
size of, 176
social media presence of, 220
sporting events and, 94, 111–114, 127–128, 151
technology adopted by, 63–65, 80–81, 146, 216, 220
timeline, iv–v
training program for, 82–83, 92, 109, 146–147, 179–182, 216
on TV, 65–66, 86–87, 131
website for, 132, 215, 220, 246
women's movement and, 79–80
Jazzercise (record album), 90
Jazzercise: A Fun Way to Fitness (book), 67, 86, 90
Jazzercise Apparel, 66–67, 130, 215, 218
Jazzercise Centers, 122, 219
Jazzercise Dance for Life, 197
Jazzercise GirlForce, 199, 239

Jazzercise instructors:
charitable giving by, 194–199, 202–207
company support for, 85
customer experience and, 163
delegating classes to, 59–62
market changes and, 217–218
number of, 67, 81
number of students taught by, 154
performance metrics for, 176, 177
selecting, 82, 145–146
training for, 61, 82–83, 109, 146–147, 179–182
Jazzercise International Instructors' Convention, 90–91
Jazzercise Japan, 128–130
Jazzercise Live, 136
Jazzercise on Location, 135–136
Jazzercise President's Club, 134
JazzerGym/Studio, 71
Jazzertogs, 66, 70, 71
Jeanne Jurad Dance Studio, 4
Jefferson, Thomas, 149, 240
JM DigitalWorks, 132, 214, 218
JM Television Productions (JMTV), 70–72, 132
Jobs, Steve, 102, 105, 106, 110, 252
Jones, Brad, 214
Junior Jazzercise, 84, 137, 206

Kagei, Tomiko, 130
Kennedy, John F., 233, 240
Kids Get Fit program, 136–138, 198–199
King, Martin Luther, Jr., 240
Kinney, Jan, 86
Knight, Phil, 110
Kovacevich, DeeDee, 68, 95–97, 100
Kroc, Ray, 151
Kurner, Kristianne, 200

Laloux, Frederic, 141–142
Langley, Sandra, 123, 124, 130
Leavitt, Joan, 5, 6, 9–14, 17, 23, 161
Leinenkugel, Jake, 98, 99
Leinenkugel, Peggy, 68, 98–100
Lincoln, Abraham, 108
Luxton, Cindy, 66, 96

Maas, Lynn, 203
MacGyver, Mary Nuckles, 86–87, 131
management style, 142–144
Mandela, Nelson, 165
Mangano, Joy, 35–36
manners, in customer service, 164–165, 172
market:
    changing, 217–218, 223
    fitting product to, 102, 129
Marshall, Patti, 196–197
Marston, Ralph, 144
Mascarenaz, Diana, 185–186
McCarthy, Young, 213
McKenzie, Cathy, 100
Mead Johnson, 132, 217–218
Meilach, Dona Z., 86
mentors:
    Joan Leavitt as, 9–14
    June Nelson Sheppard as, 6–8
    role of, 3
merchandising, 66, 71–72, 129, 135
Meyer, Danny, 224–225
microphones, 64–65
Microsoft, 35
Miller, Nikki, 60, 85, 96
mind expansion, benefits of, 238–240, 245, 253
Mindy's Kids, 202
Miracle Mop, 35–36
Miranda, Lin-Manuel, 240
Missett, Brendan, 67, 70, 250–251

Missett, Jack, 18–23, 39, 42–45, 47, 63, 71, 88, 110–111, 235, 250
Missett, Judi Sheppard:
    breast cancer battle of, 249–250
    California move by, 42–44
    career beginnings of, 16–18, 22–23, 26, 34–35
    as choreographer, 22–23, 45, 62, 100, 213
    college years of, 14–20
    courtship and marriage of, 19–23
    customer interaction with, 184, 218–219, 243
    early life of, 3–5
    as entrepreneur, 23, 35–36, 78, 81, 169, 170, 221
    financial independence of, 26
    firing of, 46–47, 53
    fitness of, 27–29
    high standards of, 153–154
    hypermobility of, 10–11
    as majorette, 10–12
    mentors of, 6–14, 43
    as negotiator, 120, 125
    note to granddaughters from, 255–256
    pregnancies of, 22–23, 67, 90
    responsibility delegated by, 59–62, 84
    as teacher, 7–8, 12, 29–33, 35, 39–41, 45, 48–52, 58
    TV appearance by, 65–66
    vocal chord problem of, 58–60
Missett, Kathy, 151
Missett, Sandra, 151
Morris, Barbara, 100
Morrison, Jenet, 169
Mozart, Wolfgang Amadeus, 252
musculoskeletal system, 236–237
musicality, 57
MYCAL (Japan), 128

National Baton Twirling Association, 11, 12
National Fitness Month, 136
National Physical Fitness and Sports Month, 198–199
negotiation:
    with bureaucracies, 124–125
    as critical skill, 54, 119, 139
    cross-cultural, 128–130, 139–140
    flexible no in, 126–131
    hard yes in, 121–123, 130
    win-wins in, 54, 119, 121, 125, 139
Nelson, Axel, 14
Nelson, Shanna Missett, 23, 27, 39, 43, 92, 96, 110, 116, 126, 136–137, 213, 218, 220, 236, 250
Nelson, Sienna, 255
Nelson, Skyla, 255
new-product development cycle, 212–215, 226
New Village Arts (NVA) Theatre Group, 200
NFL, 94, 111, 127–128
Nike, 110, 132, 217
North County Times (Oceanside, CA), 43, 50
Northwestern University, 13–16, 18, 20–22

Obama, Michelle, 199
Olympics (1984), 111–114, 127, 151
Ore-Ida potatoes, 132, 217
outsourcing, 61–62

pain, alleviating, 235–236
Pariser, Leonard, 67–68
Parker, Charlie, 232
Parker, Katie Gordon, 109
People Company (Japan), 128, 129

performance assessments:
    of customer satisfaction, 182–189
    for employees, 176–182, 190–191
physical fitness:
    benefits of, 231–238, 245
    as changing industry, 217–218
    for children, 84, 136–138, 198–199
    dancing and, 27–29, 143
    gender and, 27–29
    interest in, 80
    origins of, 107
Picasso, Pablo, 215
Pitruzzello, Toni, 179–182
"PM/Evening Magazine" (TV show), 87
Post, Emily, 164
Powell, Colin, 112
The Power of Half (Salwen), 240
practice, importance of, 152–154
President's Council on Physical Fitness and Sports, 95, 137
public relations, 86–87
Puerto Rico, 18–19

Quaker Oats, 218

Rakow, Barrie, 100
Ramey, Baby Huey, 20
rebranding, 219
recessions, 133–135, 219
Redmon, Molly, 207
Red Oak, Iowa, 4–5
Red Oak High Dancing Majorettes, 11
Reinventing Organizations (Laloux), 141–142
resistance, overcoming, 51–54
Rilke, Rainer Maria, 251
risk taking, 44
Ritter, Judy, 88
Roberts, Tim, 196

Rodriguez, Rosa, 188–189
Rogers, Will, 162
role models, 240, 253
Roosevelt, Eleanor, 148
Ruiz, Mindy Brown, 202

Sakai, Keina, 206
Sakai, Maya, 206
Salvatore, Patty, 196
Salwen, Kevin, 240
Sanford, Betty, 93
Save the Tatas Dance-a-Thon,
    197–198
Schafer, Robyn, 94, 195
Schwarzenegger, Arnold, 136
Schweitzer, Albert, 179
senior citizens:
    benefits of exercise for, 235
    Jazzercise programs for, 199
sex life, benefits of exercise to, 237
Shake Shack, 224
Sheppard, Del, 5, 43, 120–121
Sheppard, June Nelson, 6–8, 11,
    13–14, 23, 43, 81, 120, 126,
    241, 248
Sherk, Marta, 93
Shofner, Susan, 197–198
Shore, Dinah, 65, 66, 86, 87, 131
Sinatra, Frank, 252
Sinatra, Rich, 214
Singer, Andrea, 197
Sipe, Brian, 93, 94, 195
Sipe, Jeri, 68, 93–94, 100, 194–195
sleep, improving, 236
Slick, Grace, 238
Smuckers, 132
social media:
    customer engagement via, 159
    negative feedback on, 186
    performance assessment via, 176
    promotions via, 111–112
social responsibility, 194, 208

Sonnhalter, John, 48
Soroptomist Club (La Jolla, CA),
    45–46, 48
spirit, connecting to, 241–243, 245
Stabile, Allison, 214
Stanton, Elizabeth Cady, 253
Stanton, Margaret, 34, 62, 66, 79,
    81, 134
State of Women Summit (2016),
    239
Statue of Liberty rededication
    celebration, 152
Steinem, Gloria, 100
Stone, W. Clement, 177
Strausbaugh, Barbara, 100
The Studio (Jazzercise interactive
    learning management system),
    154–155, 180
success, defining, 245
Sugano, Eri, 206
support network, 54
Sweat2Smiles, 204
Sweeney, Kelly, 163, 164, 166
Szekely, Deborah, 45–47

Tart, Nicholas, 78
technology:
    for company communications, 89
    company innovation and, 216
    investing in, 74–75
    for Jazzercise classes, 62–65
    as success factor, 80–81, 102
    support staff for, 146
TED talks, 239
Thumbs Up Club (Chicago),
    19–20
Tibbels, Mary Jean, 11
Tierney, Chelle, 96
training:
    by exemplary employees,
    179–182, 190–191
    hiring practices and, 146

training (*Cont.*):
   online, 216
   standardizing, 82–83, 146–147
Tubman, Harriet, 253, 254

"Undercover Boss" (TV show), 176
Union Square Café, 224
Union Square Hospitality Group, 224
United Cerebral Palsy (UCP) of
   Greater Cleveland, 94, 195

values, business alignment with,
   150–152, 155–157, 171
Verbrecken, Van, 99
Vinci, Leonardo da, 241
Virgil, 110
Viveiros, Kristie, 66

Wadsworth, Mary, 144, 207
Wallace, Joan Marie, 66, 215
Waller, Fats, 1

WBBM, 21, 22, 42
weight control, 234–235
West, Elizabeth, 162, 167
Widerstrom, Jennifer, 168
Wiggins, Cheryl, 100
Williams, Connie, 65–66
Wolf, Katrina, 86
Wolper, David, 152
women:
   empowerment of, 239
   suffrage movement, 253
Women Presidents' Organization,
   239
women's movement (1970s), 79
Wozniak, Steve, 110

Yap, Christina, 204
Young and Beautiful Charm
   Camp, 12

Zuckerberg, Mark, 102, 240

ABOUT THE AUTHORS

Judi Sheppard Missett is a fitness and business icon, having grown Jazzercise, Inc., from a class of 15 women in 1969 to today's largest dance fitness company in the world, with cumulative gross sales topping $2 billion.

Dancing since the age of 3, Judi turned her passion into a successful career as a professional performer and choreographer. At age 25, however, she discovered her purpose—blending the art of dance and the science of exercise to make dance fitness accessible and fun for everyone. Five decades later, Judi and her daughter, Shanna Missett Nelson, continue to manage and motivate 8,500 Jazzercise franchisees to achieve their dream of independent business ownership, who in turn inspire millions of customers worldwide to live happier, healthier lives through fitness. In addition, Judi created Jazzercise Apparel, a division that generates $5.8 million in sales of branded studio-to-street apparel, and JM Digital Works, which produces award-winning video content for Jazzercise media.

As CEO, Judi's daily routine still includes choreographing and teaching the program she invented, inspiring both her corporate employees and franchisees, and mentoring other female leaders through her Platinum Membership in the Women Presidents' Organization.

In addition to two previous bestselling books—*Jazzercise: A Fun Way to Fitness* and *The Jazzercise Workout Book*—Judi has produced seven gold and platinum workout videos and three bestselling fitness albums. She and her fellow Jazzercise instructors have also raised over $30 million for a wide range of charitable organizations.

Judi has received numerous national awards and recognitions such as: the Harriet Alger Award for Entrepreneurship presented by *Working Woman* magazine, a Presidential Commendation for Top Woman Entrepreneur, four fitness Hall of Fame inductions, the Lifetime Achievement Award from the President's Council on Fitness and Sports, Entrepreneur of the Year Award from the National Foundation for Women Legislators and Empowered Women, the IDEA Lifetime Achievement Award, the Committee of 200's Entrepreneurial Champion Luminary Award, and the President's Award from Women Presidents' Organization for the No. 1 Woman-Owned Business.

In 2017, Judi spearheaded Jazzercise, Inc.'s *GIRLFORCE* initiative that offers free classes to young women of ages 16–21. The idea came to her after attending the United State of Women conference at the White House in 2016. Then-President Barack Obama and First Lady Michelle Obama encouraged a select group of businesswomen to help young women succeed. "With *GIRLFORCE*, we hope to support young women in creating healthy habits," Judi explains. "As a woman who has raised a daughter and now has granddaughters, it's important to me to support the growth and development of strong women in our culture."

Susan Carol McCarthy is the author of three novels: her debut novel, *Lay That Trumpet in Our Hands*, winner of the Chautauqua South Fiction Prize; *True Fires*; and *A Place We Knew Well*, winner of a Royal Palm Literary Award. *Lay That Trumpet in Our Hands* has been widely selected by libraries and universities for their One Book, One Community and Freshman Year Read programs. Her nonfiction *BOOMERS 101: The Definitive Collection* was a joint project between AARP and Washington D.C.'s Newseum and won a 2015 Independent Publisher (IPPY) Award and National Mature Media Award. *Building A Business with a Beat* is her second venture into nonfiction, "made every bit as compelling as fiction," Susan says, "by Judi's remarkable character, lifelong passion, transformative purpose, and truly indomitable spirit."